The Story of
IRVING BERLIN

BY DAVID EWEN
in this same series

THE STORY OF GEORGE GERSHWIN

TALES FROM THE VIENNA WOODS:
The Story of Johann Strauss

HAYDN: *A Good Life*

DAVID EWEN

The Story of
IRVING BERLIN

Illustrated by Jane Castle

NEW YORK: HENRY HOLT AND COMPANY

LE OF CONTENTS

3235- 2

FOREWORD

THIS is the story of an American composer who wrote a thousand popular hits, some so beautiful they belong among the great songs of our time.

But this story is much more.

It is the saga of a success such as few, if any, musicians have known; the saga of an immigrant boy, Israel Baline, who arrived penniless in the New York slums from a Russian ghetto, and became Irving Berlin —one of the great men of our generation, showered with the fame and wealth reserved for destiny's elect.

His is the story not of one man, but of an entire epoch. His thousand songs mirror the social history of our country during the past half century. In them the subtlest nuances of what we thought, and felt, have been magically caught.

Harold Clurman put it well when he wrote in *The New York Times* of July 3, 1949: "Irving Berlin's genius consists not so much in his adaptability to every historical and theatrical contingency, but rather in his capacity to discover the root need and sentiment of all our American lives." In discovering this "root need and sentiment of all our American lives," Irving Berlin has been to this country what Jacques Offenbach was to Paris and Johann Strauss, the younger, to Vienna a century ago. In his music there is not only tonal magic, there is a social history of our times.

Chapter One

A LAND THAT'S FREE

IF IT HAD BEEN ENTIRELY UP TO HIM,
Moses Baline would have remained the rest of his life
in Temun, a little town in Siberian Russia where his
roots were firmly planted. True, there was persecution
from time to time, and Moses knew its terrors. Cossacks would swoop down on the Jews of Temun like
some implacable fate, bringing death and destruction

on a poor and simple people whose only crime was to worship God in a synagogue instead of a church. But, as Moses Baline frequently philosophized in more peaceful times, persecution had been the lot of Jews for generations. The sufferings his ancestors had borne so heroically, he, too, could face with stoicism, strengthened by his faith in God's wisdom and purpose.

A simple man, he asked little from life that his synagogue, his religion, his huge holy tomes—and, to be sure, his family—could not provide. Measured in terms of material wealth, Moses Baline was poor indeed. By profession he was a cantor in the local synagogue, with an income hardly adequate to buy all the necessities of life for his large family. But like his father before him, and his grandfather before that, Moses never counted his blessings in currency but only in spiritual values. In spite of his poverty he felt that God had been good to him. His holy books brought him an inexhaustible wealth of inspiration and moral strength. He was a man respected in his community. His profession—singing the sad, sweet prayers of his race in the House of God—brought him close to Him, almost in direct communion.

Besides spiritual blessings, there were physical ones, too: a devoted wife with two industrious hands and an indomitable spirit, who had borne him eight children, every one a joy to his heart. They filled his home with warmth, laughter, and the vitality of new life. And every one of them dutifully obeyed his religious teaching. They would not bring shame to his respected name; they were sure to be a solace and comfort to his old age.

Often did Moses count his blessings, and find them bountiful indeed. But especially on Friday evenings did he feel himself one of the elect.

As dusk descended, he chanted for his congregation the joyous prayers honoring the approach of the holy Sabbath. Then, together with his children, he marched home—his head high as a proud man's should be—to dinner. The candles glowed benevolently on the feast his good wife had spread (a feast that more than compensated for frugal meals the rest of the week). The soft, flickering light seemed to touch his humble room almost with radiance and grandeur. Around him was his family, dressed in their Sabbath best, their faces shining with cleanliness. Then, the meal over, he of-

3

fered a prayer of gratitude to God for all the good He had brought them.

His own gratitude came from an overflowing heart. What matter, indeed, if other men had wealth, property, power? *He* had spiritual peace—and did not the holy Talmud say that this was more precious than pearls? What matter if others lived in palaces of marble? *He* had all that man requires for the sustenance of mind and body—and, in addition, he was a king in his own realm.

Many an evening, Moses Baline's wife brought him tidings of friends, neighbors, or relatives who had migrated to the New World called America. Most of them had prospered there. Work in America seemed plentiful, wages fabulous in contrast to Temun. There were other wonders as well: huge cities of stone and steel, greater even than Warsaw or Vienna; free schools for the children; freedom to worship God without the shadow of persecution; inexhaustible opportunities for self-advancement and success.

As Moses listened to these recitals, the tips of his fingers played with the end of his scraggy beard. The news from America was good—no doubt about it! And yet it did not stir him. For in his heart he knew that God was in Temun as well as in America.

On one occasion, Leah took the courage to tell him what was on her mind. She was grateful to God for all the good He had brought them in Temun—of course. But she was not thinking of herself. It was her children that were the major concern. Schools for them, an opportunity for them to learn, to become people of consequence, to grow up in cities that had no ghettos—this was something she could not help dreaming about!

Moses drew a snuffbox from his pocket, and with the tips of his forefingers and thumb lifted a few grains of snuff to his nostrils. Then he sneezed.

Slowly his mind revolved the things Leah was saying. Perhaps what Leah said had some elements of truth. Perhaps. . . But this Moses knew, too. Men became great for what they carried in their hearts and in their heads. After all, Temun had had wise men and good men, men of God. No man had to travel thousands of miles to find greatness in himself; the greatness in him must sprout and blossom, even if he lives in a wilderness.

5

Gently, Moses told this to Leah. And Leah remained silent. She was not a woman to argue with her husband, whom she respected and even feared a bit. Besides, he had spoken the truth.

Moses and Leah Baline and their eight children would probably have remained in their little town to their dying day, living simply, serving God humbly and reverently, asking little for themselves. But destiny intervened. One terrible day, early in 1892, Cossacks descended on Temun without warning. Some galloped through the narrow streets of the ghetto, brandishing their sabres, killing and wounding the poor Jews. Some put torch to the houses, shouting with delight as the flames leaped up. Others ransacked the synagogue and trampled on the holy books of the Torah. Killing, pillaging, burning a Jewish town was but sport for the Cossacks.

Somehow the Balines escaped from their homes before the sweeping tide of the Cossacks engulfed them. Together with some of the neighbors, they ran to the outskirts of the town. There, cowering under a blanket in the fields, they saw the smoke rise from their town. Ever so faintly they heard the anguished voices of the stricken townspeople. For what seemed hours they remained in hiding—terrified that the Cossacks might find them, too. But the Cossacks tired of their sport and rode out of Temun without searching the fields. The Balines were saved.

That day, under that blanket in the fields, Moses Baline knew he could stay in Temun no longer. *He* could bear their suffering, but he could not doom his children, and their children after them, to live with death and terror as perpetual neighbors.

Chapter Two

LITTLE OLD NEW YORK

THE STEAMSHIP QUIVERINGLY NUDGED
the side of a pier on the Battery, in New York City,
bringing to an end the Balines' long and anxious journey. Weeks of travel across half Europe, sometimes in
creaking wagons, more often in dusty train compart-
ments, with many a hectic stopover in bug-ridden

hotels. More weeks in overcrowded and stifling bunks in the hold of the ship, as they crossed the Atlantic.

And now, at last, America.

Many a time during the preceding month Moses Baline had looked forward to this journey's end. Many a time he had longed for the peace and quiet of a settled home. Many a time his thoughts had winged ahead toward this promised land.

Yet now that the much-dreamed moment had come, he did not experience any exhilaration. Far from it! More than ever before in the past weeks he felt a terrifying sense of loneliness. With an exquisite pang he realized that the deed was done: he had left his world behind him, with all its precious associations, all its tender memories—*forever*. Forever—the word seared like a burning iron. Suddenly he felt too old, too weary to find a place for himself in this new, strange world.

On the pier people rushed madly in all directions, amid a deafening hubbub of noise. Instinctively Moses drew his wife and children closer to him, ostensibly to protect them, but actually to draw for himself some measure of security from them.

He stood for a long time, transfixed with indecision

by the disorder around him, uncertain of what next to do. And his family clung to him awkwardly, looking to him silently for the direction he was incapable of giving.

Suddenly he heard a booming, resonant voice, a familiar voice. Because it was familiar, it sounded to Moses like music.

"Blessed be the newcomers," exclaimed the voice. "Welcome to you, Moses and Leah, welcome to America!"

Even if he had not recognized the voice, Moses would have known whose it was. It was his cousin, who had arrived in America a few years earlier, and who had assured him by letter that he would be on hand at the pier to welcome the Balines and settle them in their new world.

The sight of a familiar face brought comfort and reassurance. The heavy depression that had been smothering Moses Baline was suddenly dissipated. He chuckled with pleasure at the sight of his cousin's round, smiling face. His family began talking and laughing all at once. Effusive and jovial embraces and greetings were exchanged.

"Cousin," Moses exclaimed with feigned envy. "You are indeed already an American."

Dressed in American clothes (which to the new-comers seemed the last word in elegance) he presented a graphic contrast to Moses: The New World facing the Old. The New World appeared in a tight-fitting suit of excellent cloth, a striped shirt with a stiff collar and tie, and a black derby. The Old World wore the traditional loose black smock, a round fur hat, and peasant boots.

"A few months, my dear cousin Moses, and you, too, will be a real American—you and Leah and all the children."

With an air of a man who knew all the ropes (this was not the first time he had met relatives), the cousin shepherded the Balines past the immigration authorities, collected their baggage, and led them out to the street. There his horse-drawn wagon was waiting to transport them to their new home. His brisk and efficient manner gave Moses a feeling of self-confidence. He felt a little less out of joint with these strange surroundings. And for the first time he was optimistic about the future.

As the wagon clattered over the cobblestones into the East Side, Moses—seated with his wife next to the cousin on the driver's seat—surveyed the new world around him.

Gradually his newborn optimism and self-confidence vanished. Depression returned; everywhere he saw bigness and ugliness. He did not know which terrified him more; the tall buildings crowding the sky; the smelly, noisy streets jammed full of people; or the confusing traffic of wagons, bicycles, horse-drawn trolleys, even horseless carriages! In the gutters the children stopped their loud play long enough to shout a strange word— "greenhorn"—which Moses did not understand but which he sensed was unfriendly. It was a word he would hear often in the days that followed, stamping a stranger and a foreigner.

Images of his peaceful hometown tormented him— its order, peace, serenity, security. And a question sprang forcefully into his mind: Why, oh why, had he come?

His thoughts were interrupted by the sound of sobs. His wife was in tears. He did not have to ask why. She too was frightened and homesick and filled with confusion.

He drew her tenderly toward him, and comforted her. Of course, things seemed strange and bewildering! It *was* another world in more ways than one; and in that world, they were strangers. But Moses reminded Leah that this was a better world for the children— and wasn't that all that mattered? As for them, they were not alone. They could never be alone, just so long as God would not desert them. The holy book, the *Midrash,* had wisely said that no good Jew is an alien anywhere, for wherever he goes he has God with him.

In 1892, the year the Balines arrived in America, industry was mushrooming across the country. It raised factories, sent railroads to the furthest corners of the land, created densely populated cities. With industrialization America emerged as a world power; with it, too, came some benefits for the many, and a great multiplication of wealth for the few.

But industrialization was not an unmixed blessing; not at the beginning, at any rate. For it also created

13

crowded slums, abject poverty, and the exploitation of labor. In New York City there were half a million wage earners, half of them, women and children. Of this half a million, 75,000 worked for starvation wages under the most trying conditions. Whether they were paid for piece work, or by the hour or the week, their return for a twelve-hour day of hard work, six days a week, was meager, indeed—not enough to provide the necessities of life. And they worked in poorly venti-lated, poorly lit sweatshops, and lived in overcrowded and dirty slums.

It was estimated in 1892 that more than half a mil-lion people swarmed in New York's East Side; on one block alone three thousand people made their homes. They lived in filth and dirt, fertile breeding ground not only for drunkenness, gang warfare, and crime, but also for disease and death. The death rate in the slums was four times any other neighborhood in New York! Home was a dark flat in a miserable tenement, most of the rooms without access to light or air; and rarely was there even one bathtub in an entire house.

The misery of these East Side tenements and their

inhabitants was vividly described by Jacob Riis in a book *:

Suppose we look into one, No.——Cherry Street. Be a little careful, please! The hall is dark, and you might stumble over the children pitching pennies there. Not that it would hurt them; kicks and cuffs are their daily diet. They have little else. Here where the hall turns and dives into utter darkness is a step, and another, and another. A flight of stairs. You can feel your way if you cannot see it. Close? Yes. What would you have? All the fresh air that ever enters these stairs comes from the hall door that is forever slamming and from the windows of dark bedrooms that in turn receive from the stairs their sole supply of the elements. . . .

That was a woman filling her pail by the hydrant you just bumped against. The sinks are in the hallways, that all the tenants may have access—and all be poisoned alike by their summer stenches. Hear the pump squeak? It is the lullaby of tenement house babes. In summer, when a thousand thirsty throats pant for a cooling drink, in this block, it is worked in vain. . . .

Here is a door. Listen! That short, hacking cough, that tiny, helpless wail—what do they mean? They mean that the soiled bow of white you saw on the door downstairs will have another story to tell . . . before the day is at an end. The child is dying with measles. With half a chance it

* *How The Other Half Lives* (New York: Charles Scribner's Sons, 1890.)

might have lived, but it had none. That dark bedroom killed it.

This was the setting into which the Balines were thrust. This was their new home, their world. No wonder, then, that—as they looked about them—they were at first puzzled and confused, and later oppressed, by what they found.

Their first home was a dark, damp basement flat located in squalid Monroe Street of New York's East Side. The ten Balines were crowded into three small rooms which no air or sunlight could penetrate. There were no windows looking out to the street, only air-shafts.

Within a few weeks, a slightly less cramped flat was found just around the corner, on Cherry Street, the very same Cherry Street described so vividly by Jacob Riis. The living room (which the Balines had to use for sleeping quarters) had access to air and light through windows facing the street, though the kitchen and rear bedrooms depended on airshafts. The congestion was still great, even after the oldest daughter married and moved elsewhere.

Moses Baline found little to be grateful for. The big city confused and upset him, accustomed as he was to a small town. The noise, crowds, swirling traffic, drained his nervous energy and left him exhausted. In the old country, where life had been so placid, he had his work in the synagogue, and his hours of relaxation at home with his religious books and his contemplation. The little he had earned was enough in Temun. They had been poor, of course, just as the Jewish families around them had been poor. But poverty in the old country was far different from poverty in the New World. It had never influenced their way of living or their outlook on life. When they had a little more money there were a few more comforts in the house—a few more delicacies for the table, a few toys for the children. With less money, the luxuries had to be foregone. But never did lack of money bring such miseries as it did here; never did it interfere with a pursuit of a peaceful life and of spiritual values.

In this strange, baffling country, where the price of everything was high, Moses never seemed to earn enough money to make ends meet. He took one job, then two jobs, then three at once! In the meat market

he supervised enforcement of the religious laws govern-
ing kosher meat; in the synagogue he filled an occasional job as cantor or choirmaster; in neighborhood
homes he gave children Hebrew lessons. These mul-
tiple activities took up his time and sapped his strength;
less and less could he find the time for books and meditation. And books and meditation were an indispens-
able part of the good life, for Moses.

But this was not the worst of it. After all, *his* life
was drawing to an end. Taking all things into consideration, he had few regrets. But what about his children? Their life still stretched before them. What he
saw all around him—the tough street kids, the corner
saloons, the disease and the dirt, and the omnipresent
death—filled him with apprehension. What would become of his loved ones? Out of sheer necessity four of
them already worked in nearby sweatshops after school.
For a few coins, they huddled over work benches working at beads. And when they finished this work—since
there *still* was not enough money!—they sold newspapers in the streets. When they did get home, at last,
to eat the evening meal together, they were tired and
worn; their pinched faces prematurely old. No chance

for their young bodies to grow strong with air, and light, and relaxation. No time left—nor energy either —for study to nurture their minds.

The future, Moses often said, belonged to those who prepared for it; and childhood and youth were periods for preparation. Work in sweatshops, selling news- papers in the streets, neglect of study—exhausted little bodies and undernourished minds—what kind of a future did this promise?

Chapter Three

AROUND THE TOWN

ISRAEL BALINE (ONLY IN LATER YEARS
was his name to be changed to Irving Berlin) was born
in Temun on May 11, 1888. He was four years old
when he came to this country. Of the Old World, he
later remembered very little. The most vivid image re-
maining was of the flames rising over the rooftops of
Temun as, hiding in the fields with his family, he saw

his town ravaged by the Cossacks. The trip across Europe and the ocean soon became a blurred memory—even though he carried, and still carries, a permanent memento of the ocean voyage, a scar on his forehead, inflicted in his overcrowded cabin, when a knife fell on him from the bunk above.

Thus the world of Cherry Street was all he really knew. In it he was at home, and more than held his own. He swam in the East River at the foot of Cherry Street, as ready as his friends to perform diving feats from the wharf. In the street he played ball, tag, marbles, pitched pennies, participated in mischievous pranks. Later on, when he banded with his friends to form the Cherry Street gang, he was as eager as any for a fight with opposing gangs. And in the frequent and savage battles, he was as stouthearted as the best of them, giving blows, and receiving them.

In the streets of the East Side, there was one code, and one code alone. A fellow had to have "guts"—guts to give and to take. That was all that really mattered. Israel had guts. His acceptance by the rest of the gang was complete. The fact that he was a Jewish boy from Russia and a greenhorn, and most of them were Catholics from Ireland or Italy who had been in this country much longer, did not matter.

He understood the street. Its demands on him were explicit and could be met. Its code made sense to his boyish mind. In the street he was completely at ease, ready for any contingency.

At home he was never so comfortable with his family. He knew he caused his parents anxiety by his preoccupation with the street and its rough society. Once he overheard his father complain to his mother that he did not think he would live to see the day when a son of his would play in the streets. And his mother hurried to apologize for Israel, saying that he was, after all, still very young, and would surely outgrow this childhood foolishness. But Israel's mother was concerned too, for even as she spoke there were tears in her eyes.

One talent Israel did have. From his cantor father he inherited the gift of a sweet voice, naturally meant to sing. But, to his father's horror, Israel seldom sang the poignant chants and prayers of the synagogue, nor even the sad Jewish folk melodies passed down from one generation to the next. No! Israel went in for the popular songs of the street, raising his delicate and sensitive voice in a strange mumbo jumbo: "Ta-ra-ra-boom-de-ay, Ta-ra-ra-boom-de-ay." Or in pathetic exhortations of lost love: "Many the hopes that have vanished, after the ball." Were these the kind of songs a Jewish child was meant to sing?

As the months passed—and then the years—Moses gave up the struggle to create Israel in his own image.

Moses Baline died in 1896, when Israel was eight years old. He died a melancholy man, broken in spirit by a world he could not understand.

He had never quite found his place, nor reconciled himself to its strange life. Some solace he derived from his religion and the Old-World customs to which he clung. The world outside—the world of sweatshops and child labor, of ferocious gang wars in the streets, of vulgar songs about love, a world of materialistic values where spiritual ones were altogether forgotten— remained alien to him.

Little by little, he felt that his children were being drawn away from him by alien pursuits and interests. As the years passed, he grew lonelier and lonelier. He said nothing of his unhappiness to anyone. He was not the man to complain. Besides, he believed the holy books when they said with such wisdom: "For every affliction, silence is the best remedy." But his eyes grew sadder, the muscles of his face tauter, the lines deeper.

And, as the dusk slowly descended on him, he lived entirely in his memories and in his religion.

When the Baline family completed the seven days of mourning prescribed by Hebrew ritual, it took stock of its situation. It was none too good. Moses had earned little; but the loss of even that little was a serious blow. With her usual quiet courage, Mrs. Baline insisted they would manage. They might all have to work harder, pinch a little more, deprive themselves here and there. But God would not desert them. He never had.

A sad-faced and frail little woman to whom struggle and tribulation were no strangers, she assumed her additional responsibilities with her customary strength of spirit. Together with the innumerable chores of housework she now had to keep a father's vigilant eye on the children. That was the hardest part of her job. She was not the person to impose discipline on her children: discipline always melted in the fire of her all-consuming tenderness for them.

To all her children she gave herself unsparingly. They were the center of her existence, their happiness and welfare were all that mattered. But she was particularly attached to Israel. Jewish mothers are notoriously partial to youngest sons, and she was no exception.

She worried about him. But she never nagged him. Sometimes, with simple directness, she tried to show him that—now that he was growing up—he simply had to assume certain responsibilities. She would remind him that he had the blood of scholars and holy men in his veins, that he was meant for books, for study, for religion.

As Israel listened to her, tears would come to his eyes in spite of himself. He was not an insensitive boy by any means. Much of what his mother said he did not altogether understand. But he *did* understand that somehow she felt he was failing her. He promised her eagerly that he would try his best to reform and make her proud of him. And he meant it, too.

Because he felt so close to his mother and wanted so desperately to please her, and because he simply could not change his ways or improve in his studies, Israel was seized by an overpowering feeling of inadequacy. He felt inferior to his brothers who were not only better at books and prayers, but who were also breadwinners. But he—of what possible use was he?

Every evening the Balines went through a ritual: one by one the children filed past their mother and dropped into her lap the money they had earned that day. One evening, Israel, too, joined the parade. Shyly he dropped a few pennies in the apron. Eager to assume his responsibilities in the family circle, he had that day joined his brothers in selling newspapers after school. What he made—all of it—he gladly dropped in his mother's lap.

Selling papers late one spring afternoon, he was tempted by the delightful weather to dawdle along the river. A nearby crane, loading a coal barge, went out of control, hit him, and threw him into the water. The suddenness of the fall stunned him momentarily, though he was usually a good swimmer. Another youngster dived in and helped the half-conscious Israel to safety, and an intern from a nearby hospital pumped the water out of his lungs. The few cents he had already earned remained safely clutched in his grip; even in his semiconscious state he clung tenaciously to his own precious little contribution to the family circle. That evening—as if nothing had happened—Israel was on the family line contributing his mite.

Chapter Four

I CAN WEATHER THE STORM

ONE OF ISRAEL'S GREATEST PLEASURES
was to stroll aimlessly from Cherry Street to the Bowery and—swallowed by the passing throng—penetrate
nearby Chinatown. Occasionally he would pause outside the swinging doors of a saloon, his sensitive ear
strained for snatches of song from within. And as the
doors swung to and fro he would catch hurried

glimpses of the forbidden interior: a smoke-filled room crowded with people, sitting at tables, or standing at the bar; a waiter casually walking between the tables, balancing a tray of foaming beer mugs on his palm and singing a sentimental song as he went. And when the song ended appreciative customers threw coins at the performer.

The thought occurred to Israel that this was surely the easiest way in the world of earning money. And since singing was his one talent, he decided to become a singing waiter.

One evening he confided his ambition to his mother, certain she would approve. But her face grew tense with horror. Singing *those* songs—and in saloons. The very thought made her heart shrivel within her. If Israel wished to sing, why didn't he join a synagogue choir? Then he might grow up to be a great and famous cantor, and a rich one, too! But saloons. . .

But Israel tried to win his mother over with his oozing enthusiasm. He tried to show her that it was a way of earning money, lots of money. Hadn't he seen nickles, dimes, even quarters thrown at these singers?

His mother did not answer. She sat in her chair,

silent almost transfixed. Tears came to her eyes, and her lips trembled.

"Aw, ma, you don't understand at all," he exclaimed. He wanted to help out the family with *real* money, not with just the pennies he earned by selling papers. He wanted to buy her that rocking chair she always wanted so badly. Besides, one got to meet a lot of people in those saloons, important people. Who knows, he might even land a big paying job in some high-class theater through one of them! Then, he could buy her a house, with furniture, and servants. . . .

Still she remained silent.

Recognizing at last the futility of his arguments, Israel promised his mother he would forget all about his ambitions, since she seemed so set against them.

And almost as if she had heard nothing he had said, she whispered softly, her eyes glazed with a faraway look: "A great and famous cantor—yes. A cantor like your father was in Temun. But singing those songs in saloons? What can you be thinking of, child? You have the blood of great scholars and rabbis in your veins, Israel. You must never forget that as long as you live."

Israel had promised his mother not to become a singing waiter. But it was not easy. Try as he would, he could not stop thinking about it. He did not really know what excited him more: the prospect of easy money; or the sheer joy of singing popular songs for an audience.

All-consuming ambition gave him neither peace nor rest. The pleasures of the street and his friends began to pall; he lost all zest for gang wars, games, boyish mischief. More and more he was impelled to wander along the Bowery, to loiter outside the swinging doors, to imagine himself inside, singing, singing. . . .

Finally he made up his mind to run away from home and become a singing troubadour. Some day, he told himself, he would return and shower his mother with so many gifts she would realize he had made a wise decision. Meanwhile he was old enough to make his own way in the world.

One night after supper he strolled casually out of the flat, as if to join his friends. He went empty-handed, because he did not want to arouse suspicion, and empty of pocket, since he had that evening, as usual, surrendered his last pennies to the family treasury. He would sleep anywhere at all, it didn't matter; and to-morrow morning he would surely find a job singing. Hadn't everybody told him he was a born singer?

That first night he huddled under the stairway in the hall of a nearby tenement house. Frightened by the immense darkness and stillness around him, he slept by fits and starts. It seemed an eternity before dawn came, to find him chilled and hungry. He did not know what to do, or where to go. It was much too early for job hunting. For hours he wandered from one street to the next, adding fatigue to hunger. Then came discouragement. One owner after another turned him away, some with kindness, some with derision. There was no place for a fourteen-year-old boy.

Israel was tempted to admit defeat and go home be-fore another awful, lonely night. But his pride was stronger than discomfort or fear. And there was still a shred of hope he would find something next day. At one place he was given something to eat. His energy restored, he found a bench in a nearby park to spend the night. The next day would, perhaps, bring a turn of fortune.

It did.

Making the rounds of the Bowery, he heard that Blind Sol needed a new assistant. Blind Sol was a Bowery institution, a street singer who went from one bar to another, led by an assistant. Israel had often seen him, and noticed that, because of his blindness, and because he was well known, Bowery doors were always open to him and audiences were always generous.

Israel sought out the blind singer and timidly offered his services. To the boy's delight, he was immediately accepted. Before the day ended, Israel was in the business. He led his employer around, collecting the coins they earned. When the day's work was over, Israel was the proud recipient of twenty-five cents, his share of the income.

Before many days passed, Israel joined Blind Sol in the singing. His high-pitched, delicate rendition of the sentimental ballads of the day, such as *The Mansion Of The Aching Heart,* struck a responsive chord with his audiences. The coins came more plentifully, and Israel's income grew. Some days he earned as much as fifty cents. With enough money for food, and for a cheap hotel room, Israel felt he was indeed a man of wealth.

He did not stay with Blind Sol, once he was known along the Bowery. Sometimes the famous Callahan's in Chinatown or The Chatham in Doyer Street winked at his youth, and engaged him for an evening. Saturdays he was often employed by water-front taverns.

There were other jobs, too.

The one he liked best was with Harry von Tilzer, the Tin Pan Alley composer and music publisher. Israel was paid five dollars a week to "plug" his employer's songs. Placed in the balcony of Tony Pastor's Music Hall in Union Square, Israel would rise in his seat after a stage performer had rendered a von Tilzer song, and with the limelight flushed on him, sing several more refrains of the same song. It was all made to seem spontaneous. Israel could not resist the music. One of the acts he covered was "The Three Keatons," whose youngest member was a child named Buster, later famous as a comedian in silent movies.

But there was not always work to be had. Still, he no longer doubted his ability to get along. The thought of going home defeated never re-entered his head. There had been better days before; there would be better days again. And, indeed, they were not long in coming.

Along the Bowery, Israel was known as a serious-minded, ambitious fellow who kept to himself and never got into trouble. A quiet boy, crazy about songs and singing, he was well liked. On the Bowery they said a new song was more exciting to Israel than food or drink. And so one day as Israel looked longingly at a battered piano standing neglected in the back of a café, the owner smiled and said:

"You can use it whenever you want, kid. And you don't have to ask anybody's permission."

From that time on, Israel spent every free hour at the piano, picking out accompaniments to his songs. Occasionally he tried to piece together a melody of his own. When the result was pleasing, he felt as if he had discovered gold. In a way, he had.

And then one day on the Bowery, a soft hand touched his shoulder, and he turned to see the familiar frail, wrinkled, weather-beaten face he loved.

"Why, ma!" he exclaimed, half in surprise, half in delight. For the first time he realized how much he had missed her.

"I've been looking for you everywhere, Israel," she said, without recrimination. "I want you to come home." Her soft, sad eyes were entreating.

"But, ma, I can't give all this up. I won't."

"Who's asking you to give it up, Israel? If you want this life so much you're willing to stay away from home, I won't stand in your way. Sing your songs, Israel, even if they aren't the kind I'd like to hear you sing. Work where you want to, even though saloons are no place for you. Only—come home, Israel. I've missed you terribly."

Chapter Five

WITH A BEAUTIFUL SONG

IN THE HEART OF CHINATOWN, AT 12 Pell Street, there stood a saloon named Pelham's Café. The proprietor was a big, gruff, but kindly Russian, Mike Salter by name, called "Nigger Mike" because of his dark skin.

Nigger Mike ran a pleasant saloon, and a successful one. The drinks (five cents for beer, ten for whisky and

37

gin) were generously meted out by Sulky, the bartender. The free-lunch counter was well stocked, and there was entertainment by singing waiters, and dancing to the piano of "Nick" Nicholson.

Though quite new (it had opened two years earlier, in 1904), Pelham's Café already had an enviable reputation, and a still more enviable clientele. The most famous people of the neighborhood were found there: influential politicians, and local celebrities such as the guide, Chuck Conners, known as the "Mayor of Chinatown." Chinatown's shadier elements also frequented Pelham's Café. But because they liked Nigger Mike and respected his influence with policemen and politicians, they made no trouble in his establishment.

In 1906, Israel, once more at home with his family, found his first permanent job at Nigger Mike's. His hours were from dusk to dawn. The work was hard. Israel entertained by singing popular ballads as he carried loaded trays from table to table. When business was over, he cleaned up and swept the sawdust floors. The salary was small but it was steady. More important than his pay, however, was the opportunity to sing every evening.

Because it was frequented by Chinatown's most picturesque personalities, and because it was always proper and orderly, Nigger Mike's place attracted not only the neighborhood clientele, but more prosperous visitors from uptown. It was a favorite place for slumming expeditions. Thus one day the saloon had a royal visitor: Prince Louis of Battenberg. Occupying one of the tables with his retinue, the Prince sipped champagne and listened to Israel's rendition of current ballads. Finally the royal party called for the bill, only to learn that, with typical munificence, Nigger Mike had put all the drinks "on the house."

On his way out of the saloon, the Prince stopped to tell Israel how much he enjoyed his singing, and extended him a five-dollar bill. Israel smiled appreciatively and, emulating the grand manner of his employer, refused the "tip."

Next day this dramatic exchange between a European prince and a Bowery waiter hit the newspapers. One of the members of the Prince's party had been a reporter. A long and somewhat sentimental account told how a singing waiter had, with a polite wave of the hand, refused a gift equaling a week's salary.

For the first time, Israel saw his name in print—and in an important newspaper. Of course, he could not know that this newspaper piece, which marked his own debut in the limelight, had been written by a reporter later to become famous too. The author was Herbert Bayard Swope, subsequently the editor of one of America's newspapers, the *New York World*.

It was at Nigger Mike's that Israel wrote his first song. Strange to report about America's greatest song composer, he wrote the lyric and *not* the music.

A stone's throw from Nigger Mike's was Callahan's where Israel had gotten occasional jobs in the past. Callahan tried to rival Pelham's Café in everything, and in most things ran a poor second. But in one respect he stole a march. An original song, *My Mariucci, Take A Steamboat,* was written by two of Callahan's employees: Jerry, The Waiter, and Al Piantidosi, a pianist, later famous for the song, *I Didn't Raise My Boy To Be A Soldier*. They introduced this song at Callahan's with such success that it was actually accepted for publication. And proud Callahan could be!

Who else could boast of an original song written by his employees and published by an established house?

That such prestige should come to his greatest rival, was more than Nigger Mike could bear. He insisted that his own waiters write an original song. What was more, he insisted they get it published.

Because Israel had often entertained the help with improvised parodies on the popular songs of the day, he was selected to write the words. Nick, the pianist, had to work out the melody. Unfortunately, Nick did not know how to write music. When he had pieced together a tune in his mind, Nick called on a neighborhood violinist to put it down on paper. The completed song was called *Marie From Sunny Italy:* if Callahan's produced an Italian number, Nigger Mike's would produce one too!

The patrons of Nigger Mike's were patriotically enthusiastic about the song, and after it made the rounds of Tin Pan Alley, it was published by Joseph W. Stern and Company.

For his collaboration, Israel received a royalty of thirty-seven cents. In short, the song was a failure. But its inability to duplicate in Tin Pan Alley its acclaim at

Nigger Mike's did not bother the young author. The exhilaration of fathering a *published* song was compensation enough. No longer was he just a singer, he was now also a creator. Somehow he sensed, as he held the precious printed sheet in hand, a new world was opening up. And, like a thoroughbred quivering at the bit, Israel was impatient to fling himself completely into the new world. Ideas for songs, innumerable ideas, crowded his head.

Besides stirring new ambitions, that first printed song did something else. It gave Israel a new name, a name soon to inspire the admiration and envy of Tin Pan Alley. On the cover, below a picture of a Venetian gondola, it boldly stood: "Words by I. Berlin." He was no longer Israel Baline of the East Side ghetto and the Chinatown saloon. He was a song writer knocking at the door of fame. *That* new person required a new name. I. Berlin—Irving Berlin; it came to him on a moment's inspiration. Once it was published, he decided to appropriate it legally for himself. Thus, without half realizing it, he hastily concocted the name that was some day to become synonymous with American popular music.

Having opened new horizons with the publication of his first song, Irving Berlin (as we shall call him now) felt smothered by the confining atmosphere of Pelham's Café. His trivial duties oppressed him. Now, for the first time, he knew what he *really* wanted to do: he wanted to write songs, more songs. His eyes turned uptown, to Union Square.

Union Square was no longer the home of theaters, garden restaurants, famous saloons, and song publishers that it had been in the 1890's. The center of New York's entertainment world, progressing ever northward, was now further uptown. But some of the luster of more glittering days still clung to it. On the stage of Tony Pastor's Music Hall stars of the theater world could still be seen and heard; there were still restaurants like Luchow's, where the celebrities of the theater and song world gathered. And so it was toward Union Square that Irving Berlin's now bulging ambition soared.

However, he did not leave Nigger Mike's of his own volition. Early one morning, Sulky the bartender left the place in Irving's care. Instead of sweeping the floors, or serving early-morning beer to stragglers on their way to work, the exhausted Irving slipped into a chair and fell asleep.

He was rudely awakened to find Nigger Mike shaking his shoulder. With bleary eyes, still half-asleep, Irving recognized disaster on Nigger Mike's face. Through a storm of ugly words and accusations, Irving learned that the cash register had been robbed while he was asleep.

For some time Irving had planned to leave Nigger Mike's for greener pastures. Now he need plan no longer. Destiny was here, staring him in the face. Nigger Mike fired him on the spot and told him never again to dare come into his place.

Pelham's Café was through with him. But just as completely Irving was through with Pelham's Café, through with the Bowery, Chinatown, the whole shoddy downtown world. It had served him well, and he had no regrets. But he had new worlds to conquer.

Within the next few days he found a job as a singing waiter, at Jimmy Kelly's restaurant in Union Square, a few doors from Tony Pastor's Music Hall. Irving was going up in the world, up to the heights of Tin Pan Alley.

The name Tin Pan Alley was invented in 1903 by a journalist named Monroe H. Rosenfeld (he, too, was a composer of sentimental ballads, and quite a good one!) in an article on American popular music for his newspaper, *The Herald*. Groping for an adequate title for his article, he wandered aimlessly from one song publisher to the next. At Harry von Tilzer's office he came upon an upright piano with strips of paper stuffed behind the steel strings; von Tilzer liked its wheezy guitar-like sound. As Monroe listened to the composer play, the flat panny tones suggested the title for his article. He called his story, "Tin Pan Alley"; and America's song industry acquired a name it never lost.

"Tin Pan Alley" actually was a New York street; 28th Street between 5th and 6th Avenues, to be exact. In 1906 most of the leading music publishers were located here: Broder and Schlam (who had transferred from San Francisco), Remick's (recently from Detroit), Joseph W. Stern, Charles K. Harris, Witmark and Sons (all three from Union Square), and such comparative novices as Leo Feist and Harry von Tilzer.

There the nation's songs were manufactured. "Manufactured" is the word: for songs were often produced by factory methods, wholesale, by teams of writers, composers, arrangers, and musical stenographers. Each style of song followed a rigid formula, and was created by a specialist. Not inspiration, but mass production, fierce competition, and high-pressure salesmanship produced many a song hit of 1906.

A most important cog in this song-writing machine was the song plugger. In 1906 there were no television sets, no radios, and no talking pictures to popularize new songs overnight. To bring a song to an entire nation was the song plugger's complicated job. He convinced vaudeville and musical-comedy stars, orchestra and band leaders, singing waiters, even street cleaners —in short, everyone and anyone who could render a song in public—to perform the songs of his firm. He arranged for special, and often ingenious, ways of dinning these tunes endlessly into the public's ear. Sometimes he introduced song slides in motion-picture theaters, with the words flashed on the screen, the melody rehearsed by the piano, and the audience encouraged to sing the refrains. Sometimes he planted special singers in the balconies of theaters or on restaurant floors (as Irving Berlin had been) to repeat several choruses of pieces just performed.

A good plugger was worth his weight in gold. Only a scattered few had the personal charm, the smooth sales talk, the personal connections with the show world, the resourcefulness and ingenuity to sell songs. If the plugger did his job well, his firm's songs were sung and played in every corner of the country. And the public beat a path to the nearest store to buy the sheet music. . . .

When Irving Berlin wrote and published his first song in 1906, the vogue for the sentimental ballad still dominated Tin Pan Alley. The famous songs of the "Tearful Nineties"—songs with which that decade has ever since been identified—still echoed in the theaters and restaurants: *After The Ball, Mother Was A Lady, The Picture That Is Turned Toward The Wall, The Little Lost Child, Sweet Adeline.* To this storehouse of sad songs, the 1900's contributed new tearjerkers, ever more full of sighs and sorrow, and some livelier tunes too. By 1906 four composers were the reigning favorites: Harry von Tilzer, Ernest R. Ball, Victor Herbert, and George M. Cohan.

Like Irving Berlin, Harry von Tilzer had run away from home to sing and write music. Songs erupted from him in a veritable geyser: it is said he wrote a thousand before realizing his first success. He had come to New York in 1898, with a trunkful of songs, and $1.65 in his pocket. In a desperate struggle to make ends meet, he sold all rights to *My Old New Hampshire Home* to the Orphean Music Company for $10. It ran through a million copies, but of course brought its composer no royalties. Then the company was sold and the new owners wisely took in von Tilzer as a partner. His first contribution to the new firm was *A Bird In A Gilded Cage,* which sold two million copies. By 1902 he was able to go into business for himself, and by 1906 was one of the most successful publishers in Tin Pan Alley, largely through the phenomenal sales of his own songs, such as *Down Where The Wurzburger Flows; Wait Till The Sun Shines, Nellie;* and *On A Sunday Afternoon.*

Another top song writer of 1906 was Ernest R. Ball, who that year produced one of the great successes of the decade, the sentimental ballad, *Love Me And The World Is Mine*. Ball had come to New York to work as a pianist in the Union Square Theater, and later as a song plugger for the firm of M. Witmark. In 1903 he wrote his first success, *Will You Love Me In December As You Do In May?*, with lyrics by a young man subsequently celebrated as the Mayor of New York City, James J. Walker. That marked the beginning of Ball's career. During the next ten years he wrote besides *Love Me And The World Is Mine,* such perennial Irish favorites as *Mother Machree* and *When Irish Eyes Are Smiling*.

People everywhere in 1906 were humming the supple tunes from Victor Herbert's latest operetta, THE RED MILL, then running at the Knickerbocker Theater: *In Old New York, The Isle Of Dreams,* and *Because You're You*. This rotund, genial Irishman, who loved the good life—who ate and drank, composed music, and even breathed with so much zest—had a storehouse of simple, unpretentious melodies of great charm and freshness. He had realized his first success in 1895 with THE WIZARD FROM THE NILE, eight years after arriving in this country from his native Ireland. He

solidified his position in the theater with THE FORTUNE
TELLER in 1897, BABES IN TOYLAND in 1903, and in
1905 MLLE. MODISTE with a waltz that swept the country like a tidal wave: *Kiss Me Again.*

From the theater came also the jaunty tunes of
George M. Cohan, jack-of-all theatrical trades—producer, director, author, composer, and actor all rolled
into one. Cohan did so many things it is difficult to believe he was master of them all. But he was. From his
first hit play, THE GOVERNOR'S SON, in 1901 until his
death in 1942 George M. Cohan was one of the great
names on Broadway. Already in 1906 he was at the
top of Tin Pan Alley, thanks to the contagious popularity of his *Give My Regards To Broadway* and *The
Yankee Doodle Boy* (both from LITTLE JOHNNY JONES,
produced in 1904) and *So Long, Mary* and *Mary's A
Grand Old Name* (from FORTY-FIVE MINUTES FROM
BROADWAY, in 1905).

Such was Tin Pan Alley and such were its giants in
the year Irving Berlin published his first song—and
earned a royalty of exactly thirty-seven cents.

Chapter Six

THAT MYSTERIOUS RAG

AS A SINGING WAITER IN JIMMY KELLY'S,
Berlin continued writing lyrics. His second effort,
Queenie, My Own, was set to music by a pianist who
frequented the saloon. For his third song, *The Best Of
Friends Must Part,* Berlin tried writing the melody as

well, but the effort proved so painful he decided to forego music.

Then a song and dance man came into Jimmy Kelly's one day, and asked Berlin to write a special number for an appearance he was scheduled to make at Tony Pastor's. He knew exactly what he wanted: Between songs, he would like to recite a timely, amusing ditty in Italian dialect. He would pay all of ten dollars.

At that time, an Italian marathon runner by the name of Dorando was in the news, following his sensational defeat by Longboat, an Indian. In this event, Berlin found the theme for a ballad: An Italian barber, faithful to his country, wagers everything he has on his idol, Dorando, and loses.

But once the ballad was written, the performer changed his mind. He no longer wanted a dialect piece, had no use for *Dorando,* no intention of paying the author. Berlin peddled his song at Ted Snyder's publishing house, where the general manager, Waterson, read the lyric, and said he would buy it.

"Of course," Waterson added casually, "you've written a tune for it."

Automatically, Berlin said he had, knowing he could easily find a pianist to write a melody for him.

"Very well, then," Waterson said. "Go right into the next room and dictate your tune to the arranger. When you finish, I'll pay you $25."

Mechanically, Berlin walked toward the arranger's cubicle, torn between the desire to confess his lie, and the fear of losing $25. Since *The Best Of Friends Must Part* he had felt melodies were beyond his talents. And yet, by the time he reached the arranger, the germ of a melody came to his mind, and he began to improvise a song. It wasn't particularly good, but it might do. The arranger took it down without comment.

The song was published and actually sold well, but it was some time before Berlin had enough confidence to write his own melodies. Meanwhile, the lyrics kept pouring out. His very next song, *Sadie Salome, Go Home,* with music by Edgar Leslie was his first great success. It sold 200,000 copies.

This success set Ted Snyder thinking. A man who could hit 200,000 copies was a potential gold mine and fair game for other publishers. He offered Berlin an exclusive contract as lyricist, with royalties on all his published songs, and a drawing account of $25 a week.

Twenty-five dollars a week was not much, though it was more than he earned at Jimmy Kelly's. But it was a beginning. The contract ended Irving's career as a singing waiter. While it lasted, Berlin enjoyed singing popular songs in public. But now, with the first, sweet taste of success, he was impatient to devote all his time to song writing.

Twenty-one years old, and on the doorstep of manhood, Berlin entered Tin Pan Alley confident of himself and of his future. What others in Tin Pan Alley could do, he could do better.

The year was 1909, a pivotal year in the life of the young song writer. But it was a pivotal year in the history of American popular music as well. For when Ted Snyder signed Irving Berlin's contract, he was by the same stroke of the pen, changing the whole course of American popular music.

Berlin soon proved a top notch lyricist, as one song after another flowed from his tireless pen. He had a natural flair for words, an instinctive feeling for broad comedy, a rich vein of dialect humor and parody. He put new life into the accepted formulas of Tin Pan Alley.

By 1910—only one year after he became a salaried lyricist—one newspaper reported Berlin's humorous songs "setting the country wild." The New York *Evening Journal* engaged him to write two hundred additional verses to one popular song. And the Broadway producer, J. J. Shubert, signed him and Ted Snyder, who composed most of the music for Berlin's lyrics, to appear in a show called UP AND DOWN BROADWAY singing some of their already famous songs. For their appearance they wrote a new and successful number, *That Beautiful Rag*.

Almost any little incident was enough to set his creative talent afire. One day a song writer met Berlin in a barbershop and asked him to go out for an evening of fun; "My wife's gone to the country," the song writer explained. Automatically Berlin answered, "Hooray!", then stopped dead in his tracks, and completely oblivious of his friend, began evolving a new song. *My Wife's Gone To The Country,* with music by Ted Snyder and George Whiting sold 300,000 copies.

He was now one of the most successful lyric writers in Tin Pan Alley, and could afford to rent his family a more spacious and comfortable apartment uptown. Better still, he could afford to buy his mother a handsome oak rocking chair, fulfilling the promise made years ago, when he ran away from home. And finally he could afford to buy himself a secondhand piano on which to compose (sometimes far into the night) little melodies of his own.

For as success with lyrics came to him rapidly and completely, he was already searching for new worlds to conquer. He was to conquer a new world much sooner than he dared hope—the world of ragtime.

By introducing a new style into American popular music, ragtime—nervous, raucous, undisciplined kind of music, in comparison to the sweet ballad or the musical-comedy song—created a revolution in Tin Pan Alley.

Ragtime came originally from New Orleans, where Negro clog dancing was sometimes called "ragging." It was the Negro who was responsible for its birth.

56

Syncopation (the transfer of the accent to the normally weak part of a measure) is the trademark of ragtime; and syncopation is a development of the uneven hand clapping and feet stamping with which African Negroes accompanied their singing.

After their emancipation during the Civil War, many Negroes wandered from town to town, seeking a living. Some took to singing in the streets to the accompaniment of a strumming banjo. Because there was greater tolerance for Negroes in New Orleans than any other southern city, many settled there permanently. And because New Orleans was a center for the manufacture of wind instruments, some of these Negroes took to playing the trumpet, the cornet, and the trombone.

Unable to read music, they played in an unorthodox way, and produced unorthodox music. They combined the popular idioms with their own folk style and brought a new kind of music into existence. Largely through trial and error, they achieved new tone qualities and novel rhythms. Their music was vulgar and abandoned, without inhibition. Played everywhere in

New Orleans—in the streets, at funerals, in dance halls, at sport events or picnics—this music became a part of the city.

Ragtime, as this new music was named, was not only a way of *writing* music; it was also a way of *playing* it. Some of its effects could not be put on paper, but had to be created spontaneously during actual performance. Its pioneers were, therefore, not only composers, but instrumental performers.

The first published authentic ragtime tune was Kerry Mills' *Georgia Camp Meetin',* which appeared in 1897. Two years later came Scott Joplin's *Maple Leaf Rag,* one of the early classics. But before these classics became famous, the style of ragtime itself underwent evolution, change, and development. Small ragtime bands, and highly gifted ragtime instrumentalists, continually experimented with the new idiom in the New Orleans dance halls. Performers like Buddy Bolden and Joe "King" Oliver (both cornetists), Freddie Keppard (trumpet) and Leon Rappolo (clarinet) —and many others—had a remarkable gift for fanciful improvisations, and for arriving at new effects, colors, and tone qualities. They could improvise on a simple ragtime tune for hours on end, leaving their audiences limp with emotional and physical fatigue.

Out of these brilliant improvisations, out of these trial-and-error performances, ragtime developed a new harmonic language, often acrid and piercing in sound; new rhythmic patterns, often extraordinarily complex. The unexpected was the rule rather than the exception.

It was a haphazard development, to be sure, a hit-and-miss process dependent upon the instinct and intuition of unschooled performers and untrained composers. Yet it eventually produced an idiom all its own. Its vocabulary could be found in no other music. It was to be imitated and developed by all future ragtime composers and performers, and in later years, evolved into the styles known as "hot jazz," "swing," "boogie-woogie," and "be-bop."

Although pure New Orleans ragtime did not reach the North until World War I, echoes of the new music were heard in Tin Pan Alley almost twenty years earlier. In the middle of the 1890's, the "coon song" came into fashion in New York. It combined ragtime syncopation with Negro minstrel and variety song styles. *All Coons Look Alike To Me* by Ernest Hogan, outstandingly successful in 1896, had a special "rag" accompaniment. In the same year, a "rag" pianist by the name of Ben Harney appeared at Tony Pastor's Music Hall, much to the delight of the theater's patrons. One year later, Harney published a textbook, *The Ragtime Instructor,* which (as he said in his introduction) "was the only work published, giving full instructions on how to play ragtime music on the piano."

Ragtime melodies now came more abundantly; *My Gal Is A Highborn Lady,* introduced in New York by Barney Fagan, became a tremendous success. *The Bully Song,* sung so infectiously by May Irwin in the play, THE WIDOW JONES, was equally popular. Ragtime became popular enough for Rupert Hughes, the novelist and poet, to write a long and detailed analysis of the style in *The Musical Record* of April 1, 1899. And Tin Pan Alley, ever sensitive to public demand, began to produce rag melodies on a modest scale.

But though popular for many years, ragtime did not become a national passion (or a national disease, as others preferred to describe it) until 1911. In that year, a new ragtime song was born. This song infected the entire country like an epidemic. America went ragtime-crazy.

And it went ragtime-crazy because Irving Berlin wrote a song called *Alexander's Ragtime Band*.

1900

Chapter Seven

THE SUN SHINING SO BRIGHT

RAGTIME FASCINATED IRVING BERLIN.
This fascination led him to write, for his own amuse-
ment, a piano "rag" tune, *Alexander And His Clarinet*.
He liked the piece better than anything else he had
written. But he feared it had no commercial value, de-
fying as it did the long-set traditions of Tin Pan Alley.
When Jesse Lasky (now the famous motion-picture

executive, but then the manager of the *Folies Bergères* Theater in 47th Street near Broadway) turned it down as a production number, Berlin felt his fears fully justified. He consigned the manuscript to a drawer, and to what he believed was permanent oblivion.

In 1911, the Friars Club (the famous organization for theater people) recognized Berlin's growing importance as a song writer by electing him a member. Each year the club produced a show for its members called THE FRIARS FROLIC. Berlin was invited to make a personal appearance in the 1911 production at the New Amsterdam Theater. The occasion, Berlin felt, called for something special, something off-the-beaten track, to interest professional theater folk. Suddenly he recalled *Alexander And His Clarinet,* took it out, found he still liked it, and wrote a lyric. Retitled *Alexander's Ragtime Band,* he himself introduced it. It was well received. And then forgotten.

Not long after THE FRIARS FROLIC, the song was played in a humble New York theater in THE MERRY WHIRL. Once again it pleased the audience, and once again it was forgotten. Then the famous vaudevillian, Emma Carus, sang it in Chicago with all her customary *zou gotta sell it!*

verve and animal spirit. She brought down the house. By the time her run was over, she had the entire city throbbing to the rhythms of *Alexander*. "If we were John D. Rockefeller or the Bank of England," wrote one Chicago newspaperman, "we should engage the Coliseum, and get together a sextet including Caruso. . . . After the sextet sang it [*Alexander's Ragtime Band*] about ten times, we should, as a finale, have Sousa's Band march about the building tearing the melody to pieces with all kinds of variations."

This marked the beginning of the triumph of a song. From Chicago *Alexander* swept eastward and westward to blast the whole country like a typhoon. Within a few months, one million copies of sheet music were sold. In less than a year, it became the most widely sung, played, and danced-to song of the period. A nation, long conscious of ragtime music and long interested in it, became completely intoxicated with its rhythms. Ragtime was king—and largely because of *Alexander*.

Temporarily at least, the sentimental ballad lost its imperial position. Ragtime took its place. Everybody was doin' it now: writing ragtime songs, plugging ragtime songs, performing ragtime songs, and singing ragtime songs.

Besides changing the song style so long ascendent and so long slavishly copied in Tin Pan Alley, *Alexander* worked another revolution. As one writer aptly remarked, it changed the social habits of our country. Its impulsive, irresistible rhythm not only quickened the pulse and the heartbeat; it made feet tap too.

Social dancing had not been much of a pastime before 1911. Whirling dances like the polka, the waltz, the schottische, required considerable stamina; only the young had the endurance. Fifteen-minute rest periods were necessary between dances. Midweek dancing was unheard of; it was much too enervating for working days.

But ragtime, with its even 2-4 and 4-4 rhythm, brought to social dancing a simple walking step requiring neither physical endurance nor complicated training. The old could now dance as well as the young; the novice, as well as the initiate. Dancing, far from being physically exhausting, was relaxing; it could even be indulged in weekdays.

With *Alexander* bringing the dancing itch to feet

old and young, and with ragtime rhythm simplifying steps so that all could dance, the country suddenly became dance mad. Hotels and restaurants in the large cities, introduced dancing with meals, and special tea-dances in the late afternoon. Respectable businessmen slipped away from their work in midafternoon to join their wives for an hour of the turkey trot. The demand for after-theater dancing brought about the origin of the night club, first Lee Shubert's *Palais de danse,* followed by William Morris' competitive *Jardin de danse.* An evening's entertainment consisted in going from one hotel to the next, and then to different night clubs, on a veritable dancing spree. And those who remained at home took up parlor dancing instead of singing popular songs around a piano.

Everybody was dancing to the strains of ragtime; from the glamorous Vernon and Irene Castle (whose varied dance creations to the one-two step of ragtime were overnight sensations) to factory workers enlivening lunch hour with the one-step, two-step, turkey trot, bunny hug, grizzly bear, tango, and fox-trot. The newspapers revealed that John D. Rockefeller was taking private dancing lessons; and that Mrs. Stuyvesant Fish

—appalled by the demoralizing nature of the new dances, yet unable to avoid them at her functions—had commissioned the Castles to originate a more discreet dance, The Innovation. People died while dancing—one of them a man, one hundred years old; colleges barred dancing altogether (Yale) or sanctioned it pontifically (Harvard). The Pope officially expressed his disapproval. Ministers denounced it. One society lady tried to use her influence to pass a law in Washington forbidding it.

But America kept on dancing.

Not only dancing itself, but the music that brought on the new madness, was the subject of intense passionate controversy. A spirited battle was fought in the name of ragtime between those who felt that it was a native musical expression deserving serious attention and encouragement, and those who denounced it as vulgar, and a degradation of all musical and moral values.

Representing the first group was the editor and critic, Hiram K. Motherwell. He wrote in the *Seven Arts Monthly,* July, 1917:

To me, ragtime brings a type of musical experience which I can find in no other music. . . . I like to think that it is the perfect expression of the American city, with its restless bustle and motion, its multitude of unrelated details, with its underlying rhythmic progress towards a vague Somewhere.

The composer, teacher, and writer, Daniel Gregory Mason, who belonged in the opposing camp, bellowed in the *New Music Review* in the year 1917:

Nonsense! Ragtime . . . is . . . no creative process. . . . It is a rule of the thumb of putting a "kink" into a tune that without such specious rehabilitation would be unbearable. It is not a new flavor, but a kind of curry or catsup, strong enough to make the stale old dishes palatable to unfastidious appetites.

Perhaps the most prophetic tribute ragtime received came from England, the writer being an anonymous contributor to the London *Times* in 1913:

Of ragtime, there can be no doubt that it is absolutely characteristic of its inventors. From nowhere but the United States could such music spring. It is the music of the hustler and of the feverishly active speculator. . . . We look to the future for an American composer—not, indeed, to the Parkers and the MacDowells of the present who are taking over a foreign art, ready-made, imitating it with more or less success, and with a complete absence of vital force, but to someone as yet unknown, perhaps unborn, who will sing the songs of his own nation in his own time and of his own character.

Critics might rave and fume—as, indeed, they did; denunciations might thunder from the pulpits; the American Federation of Musicians might demand a boycott. But nothing and no one could stem the tide of ragtime's popularity, now that *Alexander* was its eloquent spokesman.

For in its subtle pulse, ragtime caught the spirit of the times, the quickening tempo of life. The horse-drawn trolley had been replaced by electric tramways; subways were racing beneath the surface of American cities. Two hundred thousand motorcars, produced in 1910, brought new speed to country roads as well as city streets. Railroads streaked across the country at mile-a-minute speed. And the first successful experiments in travel through air forecast a dizzy future.

The leisurely gait of the nineteenth century had given way to the throbbing rhythm and movement of the twentieth, a rhythm and movement which music like ragtime, and a song like *Alexander's Ragtime Band,* expressed in popular terms.

69

Perhaps no other song of our generation made as indelible an impression on American life as *Alexander's Ragtime Band*. Its success was no flash in the pan. Through the years, its popularity has persisted, its importance has grown. It is one of the classics in American popular music, with an appeal that refuses to die. Ragtime has come and gone, but *Alexander* has survived.

Twelve years after its composition, a famous concert artist, Eva Gauthier, gave a recital in Aeolian Hall including songs by the foremost contemporary composers (Schoenberg, Milhaud, Bartók, Hindemith) and by old masters (Purcell, Byrd, Bellini). One of the groups in her recital was devoted to American composers, and one of the songs was *Alexander's Ragtime Band*.

Fourteen years after its composition, the novelist Carl van Vechten wrote in *Vanity Fair,* March, 1925, that *Alexander* was "real American music—music of such vitality that it made the Grieg-Schumann-Wagner dilutions of MacDowell sound a little thin, and the saccharine bars of *Narcissus* and *Ophelia* so much pseudo-Chaminade concocted in an American back-parlor, while it completely routed the so-called art music of the professors."

On February 12, 1924, the popular orchestra leader, Paul Whiteman, gave his historic all-jazz concert at Aeolian Hall, New York. He wanted to prove that American popular music had a significant contribution to make. Heard for the first time was George Gershwin's now historic *Rhapsody In Blue*. Another piece on that program—representative of the best that popular music had thus far produced—was *Alexander*.

Twenty-seven years after it was written, *Alexander's Ragtime Band* gave its name to and was featured extensively in a motion-picture cavalcade of Irving Berlin's hit songs. Revived in 1938, the song became a nation-wide hit again.

And a few years later *Alexander* acquired new stature and dignity, when Robert Russell Bennett, the American composer, made a symphonic arrangement, since performed by several major American orchestras.

The sweeping success of *Alexander's Ragtime Band*, and the new craze for dancing it provoked, brought a veritable deluge of ragtime songs from Tin Pan Alley.

Fittingly enough, the most successful—and the best—were written by Irving Berlin. As he was to do again and again in his career, Berlin had completely absorbed a popular idiom, and, through the subtle chemistry of his melodic genius, transformed it into a style so personal that it almost seemed he had invented it. In rapid succession he produced a number of smash hits that intensified the ragtime fever and set a standard few could duplicate. *That Mysterious Rag . . . Whistling Rag . . . Ragtime Violin . . . Everybody's Doin' It . . . Everybody Step.* He was now—no question about that—the king of ragtime. And that regal position he was to maintain for the next few years.

Two illustrative anecdotes demonstrate the now dominating role he filled in ragtime music.

Elsie Janis, the brilliant vaudeville star, had come back from London infected with the ragtime disease by tunes she had heard in London, aboard ship, and during her first few days in New York. Meeting Berlin at a party, she hummed a snatch of one ragtime melody and asked him if he knew it. Berlin answered her by sitting down at a nearby piano and playing the entire song. She hummed a few bars from another one. Berlin played that, too. When Berlin had gone through half-a-dozen melodies from Elsie Janis' clues, she said in amazement, "You certainly have the most phenomenal memory I've ever encountered!" Berlin did not explain that he knew the songs because he had written all of them.

The second anecdote takes us to London in 1913, where Berlin, billed as THE RAGTIME KING, was appearing at the Hippodrome Theater. He sang a few of his most famous ragtime songs, including—to be sure!—*Alexander's Ragtime Band*. He also introduced *That International Rag,* finished in the late hours of night before his appearance! "When I asked the audience," Berlin later related, "what other songs of mine they would like to hear, they shouted, *'Robert E. Lee,' 'Kitchy-Koo,'* and several others I had not written. . . . They thought I wrote every ragtime song they'd ever heard."

No less indicative of Berlin's growing fame was a call from the dapper Florenz Ziegfeld, one of Broadway's most successful producers.

Florenz Ziegfeld had entered show business as the

manager of Sandow, the strong man. But he was ambitious for bigger things. He wanted to produce musical shows on Broadway—shows that glorified more stars, exploited more beautiful chorus girls, and utilized more lavish sets than ever before. Provided with funds by another showman, William A. Brady, Ziegfeld imported to New York in 1896 a dazzling French singing actress, Anna Held, and around her built a sumptuous musical comedy, THE PARLOR MATCH. It opened on September 21, and was—as Ziegfeld knew it would be—a sensation. Anna Held became the talk and the toast of the town. And Ziegfeld established himself as the country's foremost impresario of musical comedies. When he presented Anna Held in her second American play, THE LITTLE DUCHESS, the first week of ticket sales broke all existing records. Then Ziegfeld evolved the idea for a magnificently mounted revue to be called THE ZIEGFELD FOLLIES. The success of the first edition, in 1905, inspired him to make it an annual event. The FOLLIES became a national institution setting the standard for the production of musical shows.

Besides the FOLLIES, Ziegfeld also produced a lavish

midnight musical revue on the roof of the Amsterdam Theatre. It was for this revue, called JARDIN DE PARIS, that Ziegfeld wanted Berlin's collaboration. The stars were dancer Bessie McCoy and comedian Leon Errol. The music had been written by Maurice Levi and Raymond Hubbell, but, as Ziegfeld told Berlin, a few additional numbers were still needed. Berlin handed him the best of his recent songs, and from them the producer selected four: *Ephraham Played Upon The Piano, You've Built A Fire Down In My Heart, Doggone That Chilly May,* and *Woodman, Woodman, Spare That Three.* And on June 26, 1911, the opening night of JARDIN DE PARIS, Berlin made his official bow as a composer for Broadway. Characteristic, indeed, was it that the first Broadway revue for which he wrote songs was one of the season's hits.

Such unequaled success as Berlin now enjoyed naturally invited envy. And envy is the father of malicious rumor. To discredit Berlin's achievement a silly story was circulated around Broadway (and for a while was actually believed!) that he did not write his own songs. They said he had bought *Alexander's Ragtime Band* from a little Negro boy for $10. When *Alexander* be-

75

came successful, rumor maintained, Berlin took the boy into his employ and ever since then it was the little fellow—and not Berlin—who actually wrote all those magnificent hits. As Berlin continued to follow one success with another it became apparent—even to the most skeptical—that the little Negro boy was too much of a gilt-edge investment to remain so long invisible. The rumor died and was forgotten; but not by Berlin's friends, among whom the little Negro boy became a favorite subject for jokes. Once, when Berlin returned from a Palm Beach vacation bronzed by the southern sun, and stepped into his office, his secretary exclaimed: "Well, well! *Here* comes Berlin's little Negro boy!"

Chapter Eight

NO ONE ELSE BUT YOU

THEN, SUDDENLY, THE WONDERFUL OUT-
pouring of song was cut short by a tragedy.

In 1912, Irving Berlin married Dorothy Goetz,
beautiful sister of Broadway producer, Ray Goetz.
Their honeymoon in Cuba was idyllic. They returned
to New York exhilarated by dreams of a wonderful
life together in a home on Riverside Drive. Berlin was

bursting with ideas for songs, songs expressing his new-found happiness.

The songs were never written. Two weeks after the Berlins moved into their beautiful new apartment overlooking the Hudson, Dorothy died of typhoid fever unwittingly brought back from Cuba.

Berlin was inconsolable. He had lost the meaning and purpose of his life. Without Dorothy everything was hollow. He felt alone, terribly alone.

His brother-in-law, Ray Goetz, took him to Europe in hopes that the adventure of travel might ease the pain. The trip was a nightmare. Berlin could run away from the scene of his disaster; but he could not run away from himself. He returned to New York and tried to forget his heartache in his work. But melodies would not come. He did complete a few songs—at the expense of Herculean effort. They were stiff, formal, without his usual charm and spontaneity; and they were failures.

"I'm through, finished," he told Goetz bitterly. "If I did have any talent, Ray, it died with Dorothy."

All of Goetz' efforts to restore Berlin's confidence seemed futile. In desperation he tried a new tack.

"Why don't you give in to your grief, Irving, and work it out of your system?" he said.

Berlin looked faintly interested.

"I mean," went on Goetz, "why don't you write a song about it? You know, Irving, it might help."

Fantastic, said Berlin. Outrageous, to use his personal tragedy as material for a song. Besides, he just couldn't write about anything which affected him so personally and deeply.

"The greatest composers wrote their best music under the lash of grief, Irving," Goetz said. "You know that. And you're not different. Try it, anyway. It may work wonders. In any case, it can't hurt you any more than you already have been hurt."

Berlin dismissed the idea as ridiculous. Yet, once Goetz had gone and he was left alone, he could not altogether suppress an idea for a song ballad. A few simple lines that seemed to express his poignant sorrow: he had lost the sunshine and roses, the teardrops and dew; he had lost everything beautiful, when he lost Dorothy. The words came easily as his idea crystallized. Before he knew what he was doing, he was at the piano working out a melody.

And so he wrote the first of his great ballads, *When I Lost You.*

When I Lost You sold almost a million copies but this was not too important. More important, by using words and music as emotional catharsis, Berlin, at last, found relief. He was able to compose again, with all his old-time zest.

When I Lost You introduced Berlin as a composer of sentimental ballads, a field in which he was to become unique and incomparable. Once again, he absorbed an existing song style, and added such a wealth of subtle feeling, such simplicity and directness, such sensitivity of mood and delicacy of expression, and such sheer magic, it seemed he had actually invented the style himself.

In 1914, two years after the tragic loss of his wife, Berlin invaded another new field of activity. Although four of his songs had been successfully introduced in the JARDIN DE PARIS, Berlin had never written a complete score for a Broadway show. Then early in 1914, producer Charles B. Dillingham came to him with an idea for a lavish musical to feature the sensational dancing team of Vernon and Irene Castle, a kind of "rag-time musical comedy." Thinking of rag, the name of Irving Berlin had inevitably occurred to Dillingham. Would he write the score?

Berlin wrote thirteen numbers for WATCH YOUR STEP, not only infectious ragtime like *The Syncopated Walk*, but tender, wistful love songs like *What Is Love* and *When I Discovered You* and the humorous *I Love To Have The Boys Around Me*. The variety of pace, mood, emotion in his first theatrical score proved—for all time—that Berlin was born to write music for the theater, just as he was born to write songs of the nation.

WATCH YOUR STEP—book by Harry B. Smith and lyrics and music by Irving Berlin—began its long run on Broadway, December 8, 1914. "Berlin," wrote one reviewer, "is now a part of America." Berlin was also now a part—and an integral part—of the American theater.

To Berlin's office at Ted Snyder's there came, one day in 1916, a young man with dark, intense eyes. He wanted Berlin's opinion on some songs he had written.

The young man spoke of his ambition with sincerity and enthusiasm, and with quiet self-confidence. Berlin was attracted to him. Others had come seeking an easy formula for success; this young man did not seem at all concerned with money. Though a denizen of Tin Pan Alley, a song plugger at Remick's, he seemed sublimely unconcerned about his own sales or profits or income. He glowed with a mission: to create out of American popular music a serious American art.

The young man put it this way.

An American composer, if he were to produce something genuine and honest, simply had to use the idioms around him. Why couldn't a composer exploit the musical technique developed by the masters, and yet use a popular style? Wasn't it possible to produce something of permanent importance, something dreamed, within the limited framework of popular song? *He* wanted to write popular songs that by-passed the accepted and convenient formulas and reached for originality and artistic importance.

Berlin listened attentively. What the young man had to say made sense, no doubt about it. But it wasn't what he said, but the way that he said it, that impressed

Berlin. In just such a way must Beethoven have spoken when he dreamed of extending the symphonic form, or Wagner when he expounded his ideas about the music drama!

"Let's hear some of your songs," Berlin said.

The young man needed no second invitation. He leaped to the piano, played one number, then another, then a third.

"My boy," Berlin said. "You really have something."

"Well, Mr. Berlin, what do you advise me?" the young man asked.

Berlin grew serious.

"Look here," he said, putting his arm around the young man's shoulders, "I'm not one of your trained musicians. I can't tell a triad from a modulation. I've always written my songs from the heart, not from the head. If you're coming to me for criticism, you won't get it. I couldn't put my finger on a technical fault to save my neck.

"But I do know this. Your songs sound good. They're fresh. They're original. God knows, you've got the gift of melody. They're not the same old hash the boys keep cooking.

"The only advice I can give you is this: Keep plugging! Don't give up your standards for the sake of sales. You can't miss. And if there is any way I can help you, you know where to find me."

"That's all I wanted to know," the young man said as he rose to go. "Hearing that from you, Mr. Berlin, means a lot to me."

"Good-by and good luck," Berlin said. Then, almost as an afterthought: "But you haven't told me your name."

"My name," the young man replied, "is George Gershwin."

A few months later, young Gershwin revisited Berlin.

"I see," Berlin said in greeting, "that you're beginning to make a name for yourself."

For since their last meeting, Gershwin had published several songs, and had another in the Broadway musical, THE PASSING SHOW OF 1916. Convinced that he was now on his way, Gershwin had given up his stultifying job at Remick's, and was now looking around for a better job. Could Berlin find a place for him?

"Yes, I can," Berlin answered without hesitation. "I need a good musical secretary, and if you want the job, it's yours. The work isn't backbreaking, and will give you plenty of time for your own work. And I'll pay you three times what they gave you at Remick's."

Gershwin beamed. To work with the famous Irving Berlin! And for that privilege to be paid a fabulous salary. It was more than he had dared dream.

"Only, George," Berlin added hastily, "I hope you don't take the job."

A moment of silence.

"It's this way, George," Berlin continued. "You'd have a good job with me, sure, and you'd be earning a good salary. And I'd like having you. But you've got too much talent to be working for any other composer. You weren't meant to write down somebody else's melodies; your own are too darned good. If you worked for me, George, you'd begin thinking like me, perhaps writing like me. And that's no good. You've got to go your own way."

Gershwin pondered Berlin's argument. It made sense. Still—he needed a job badly, and he would never find a better one.

"If you still want the job," Berlin said, "it's yours. And we'll forget everything I just said."

Gershwin rose.

"I guess there's only one thing I'd rather do than work for you, Mr. Berlin. And that's to make my own way writing my own songs. You're right. I'll just have to turn down your offer, and go my own way—alone."

"George," Berlin exclaimed, "you not only have talent, but you have guts!" That combination just can't be beat. You'll go far."

Irving Berlin's faith in Gershwin was, of course, fully justified. Two years later, Gershwin composed his first smash hit, *Swanee,* which Al Jolson sang to nation-wide popularity. Then George White engaged him to write the score for his annual Broadway revue, THE SCANDALS, a worthy rival of THE ZIEGFELD FOLLIES. But Gershwin was to go beyond Tin Pan Alley and Broadway, to make musical history. In 1924 he wrote the *Rhapsody In Blue* in which the American popular idiom truly realized its artistic significance, and which has since become the most famous serious work by an American composer.

In Tin Pan Alley, where rivalries are so numerous, envy so intense, and every man jealous of his fame, the mutual admiration of Irving Berlin and George Gershwin is a refreshing, even inspiring, spectacle. To the end of his days, Gershwin was grateful to Berlin for being the first to recognize and encourage his talents, and always spoke of Berlin's melodic genius and his contribution to American popular music with humility and reverence.

"Irving Berlin," Gershwin wrote in a magazine article when he was at the height of his fame, "is the greatest American song composer. He has vitality, both rhythmic and melodic, which never seems to lose its freshness. He has that rich, colorful, melodic flow which is ever the wonder of all those of us who compose songs. His ideas are endless. His songs are exquisite cameos of perfection. Each one is as beautiful as its neighbors. Irving Berlin is America's Franz Schubert."

And Irving Berlin watched Gershwin's soaring star with no little personal satisfaction, mingled with genuine respect and awe. When George Gershwin died so prematurely in 1937, Berlin wrote a poignant lyric to honor the younger man who could "step down from the heights of grand opera to a chorus of thirty-two bars."

Chapter Nine

TO AN OLD-FASHIONED GIRL

SEATED IN THE ROCKING CHAIR HER SON had bought her with his first income as a song writer—and in the uptown apartment he had rented and furnished for her—Mother Baline revolved in her mind the miracle she had seen. It was difficult to believe it had actually happened to *her*.

During those first drab years on the East Side, she

had frequently bemoaned the fate that had brought her to this country. Those glowing reports about the wonders of the New World had seemed so much fraud. This was the land of opportunity, they said—and she saw her children in sweatshops. This was the land of free education, they said—and she saw her boy, Irving, drop his schooling to work in a saloon. This was the land where a man could carve his own future, they said —and she saw Irving living among gangsters and drunkards!

Like her husband, she had been terrified and confused; and like him, she had felt herself trapped in such a large city.

But suddenly and inexplicably the miracle took place, not to somebody else, but to her. Her boy, Irving, as he called himself (she called him Israel) was a success beyond her wildest dreams. Wealth and fame were his. The most important people in New York were proud to call him by his first name. Newspapers and magazines wrote about him, printed his picture. It was her Irving who was applauded so vociferously when he appeared on the stage of Hammerstein's; her Irving who received an ovation after the opening

Important

night of WATCH YOUR STEP; her Irving whose melodies she heard people singing in the streets!

That a poor Jewish boy born in a ghetto and raised in the slums—a boy without background, influence, or even education—could rise so high was wonder enough. But to Mother Baline it was more miraculous still. For Irving had been the source of her greatest anxieties and fears as a child; he was the one about whose future she had worried most.

Now all her anxieties and worries were laid to rest. She had every material good her heart could possibly desire. Irving saw to that. She could have more, too, if she did not resist so fiercely his every attempt to shower her with gifts. But the greatest gift her son had given her was not this apartment, or diamonds, or beautiful clothes. It was the peace that now settled in her heart, the peace that came from the knowledge that far from coming to evil, her son had come to so much good.

Only one regret stirred restlessly within her, as she sat in her rocking chair thinking her thoughts and looking vacantly out of the living-room window: That her husband had not lived to see all this come to pass.

One evening at dusk Irving burst into her apartment and asked her to put on her best clothes.

"This is an occasion, ma," he said mysteriously. "We have to go somewhere important."

"But, Israel," she cried. "It's already six o'clock, and I have to make supper."

"Supper can wait, ma," he insisted. "I've got a taxi waiting downstairs, so please hurry."

His mother clicked her tongue. "A taxi, Israel, how do you go spending your money!"

As the taxi swept them to another, and more elegant, part of the city, his mother lamented her "fancy ride in a taxi," when she should be home "making supper for the children." At last they stopped in front of a private house.

"Who do we know here?" his mother asked.

A servant welcomed them at the door. They entered and silently passed from one luxuriously furnished room to another. In the glistening kitchen the cook was preparing the evening meal. Everything was new and apparently expensive.

"Funny," his mother chuckled, "she acts as if *we* owned the place."

92

The chuckle froze in her throat as, like a flash of lightning, the truth came to her.

"Israel, my boy, my darling. What did you go and do?"

Irving tried to say many things. He tried to tell her how much he regretted the terrible trials and fears that he, as a boy, had brought her. He tried to tell her that she—who all her life had worked so selflessly for her children without ever a thought for herself—deserved gratitude and compensation far greater than he could ever give her.

He tried to tell her all these things—also, what she had always meant to him, and what she would always mean to him. But the words would not come.

All he could mutter—and it was hard for him to suppress some tears as he spoke—was: "Ma, *you* don't have to make supper no more."

"First, that rocking chair, then an apartment, and now this house," she whispered. "When you promised me these things so many years ago, Israel, I didn't think I'd live to receive them. But God has been good to me, Israel. He has given me you."

93

"And not only this house," Berlin said eagerly. "But anything else you want anything."

"There *is* something else, Israel," Mother Baline hesitated, "something that means more to me than houses or diamonds."

"You know, ma, if I can give it, you will get it."

"None of us lives forever, Israel," Mother Baline said gently. "In God's time I will be called to join papa. When that day comes, Israel, I want you to say *Kaddish*—the prayer of mourning—for me, as every good Jew must."

Before Berlin could say a word, she continued: "I know, Israel, you never did have patience for our religious customs. But you are my youngest son, and my most precious. And this one custom I want you to keep. When I die I want you to say prayers for me."

"I promise, ma."

And when, a few years later—on a hot and humid day in July of 1922—they buried Mother Baline in a Brooklyn cemetery, with the simple, devout ceremony she wanted, Irving Berlin chanted the *Kaddish* for his mother, as he had promised he would.

Chapter Ten

THIS IS THE ARMY

UNRESTRICTED SUBMARINE WARFARE launched by Germany early in 1917 inflicted a heavy toll on American shipping. As the weeks passed, it became obvious that America, so long neutral, would be drawn into the holocaust. Then on April 2, President Wilson appeared before Congress to ask for a declaration of war. Five days later, on Good Friday, America plunged headlong into the conflict.

A people who had made every effort to remain at peace now hurled its energy into achieving victory. Industry, labor, agriculture were mobilized. Huge loans were floated. Most important of all, an army was conscripted. From one end of the country to the other, and from every walk of life, young Americans poured into training camps. America was preparing to throw the full weight of her tremendous resources and man-power against the victorious enemy tide.

Irving Berlin's doctor informed him that a long standing nervous indigestion would keep him out of the Army. Eager to serve in some way he plagued Washington for an assignment to entertain troops overseas. But before the officials acted, his local draft board called him up for a medical examination. To his amazement, he was accepted for active duty.

Transplanted from his luxurious New York apartment to the bleak and crowded barracks in Camp Upton, and wearing a uniform a little too large for him, Irving Berlin went through the rough initiation to army life. He rose at dawn, an hour when, as a civilian, he had usually gone to sleep, and went to bed at the ungodly hour of nine. Accustomed to the delicacies of New York's finest restaurants, he now lined up in the mess hall, mess kit in hand, for the inevitable pork and beans. Close-order drills, inspections, K.P., latrine duty, filled the days with fatigue, or boredom, or disgust. And always—wherever he went, whatever he did —there was the perpetual bellow of a sergeant.

No special dispensation was made for America's celebrated song composer now turned rookie—even though his name and his songs were known everywhere and by everybody. On the contrary! There were some officers who, suspecting Berlin wanted special consideration (though he never asked for it) went out of their way to see that the young celebrity was treated with special roughness; they assigned him particularly dirty details.

For better or worse, Berlin was in the Army. Like everyone else, he learned to curse and gripe, and dream enviously of a softer civilian life, and, at the same time, to take the Army in his stride.

When Berlin had been at Camp Upton for several months, it changed from a training center to a temporary station for troops on their way overseas. Now proudly wearing the three stripes of a sergeant, Berlin was retained at Upton.

One day, the commanding officer, Major General J. Franklin Bell, called him in. General Bell pointed out that the troops were restless with inactivity, impatient, and concerned over their future, as they waited to be shipped overseas. What the general had in mind was a new service center where the men could relax, have some fun, and take their minds off themselves and their future. General Bell needed about $35,000 for such a center, and the money would not be provided by Washington.

"And that's where you come in Sergeant," the General added with a smile.

Would Berlin take it upon himself to produce a show, a *soldier's* show—recruiting his talent at Upton? They could present it on Broadway for a few weeks. It might possibly bring in the needed $35,000.

Needless to say, the assignment was eagerly accepted. For the time being at least Berlin was freed of the tyranny of army life, its endless drills, its laborious details. That, in itself, was a blessing to a tired soldier.

But the assignment meant something else, too—something more important. It meant that Berlin could, after all these months, return to the business he knew best —show business. He could drop his rifle and return to writing songs.

Drawing his ideas from his own experiences as a rookie, Berlin wrote the whole show himself—not only the music and the lyrics, but also the skits and ensemble numbers. He wrote out his script in longhand; and picked out his melodies on a battered camp piano. When he had a workable script, he sent out a call for volunteers. Two hundred and twenty-seven hopefuls answered, from whom Berlin selected his cast.

There followed endless grueling rehearsals as he tried to train amateurs up to professional standards. Songs, dances, skits, ensemble numbers, were gone over again, and again, and again. Scenery was improvised from the ragtag and bobtail of an army camp. The little sergeant who used to grumble at an hour's march, thought nothing of whole nights of sweat and tears.

And, at last, YIP, YIP, YAPHANK, as the show was called, was ready.

On July 26, 1918 it opened at the Century Theatre

in New York. After the opening chorus, the "Captain" appeared before his men. He told them that there was a seasoned enemy across the footlights, and that enemy was—the audience. Though it was surrounded, it still had to be riddled with jokes, songs, and dances until it surrendered. The order "to attack the audience" was given, and the men proceeded to conquer the "enemy." The cheers, the stamping of feet, the delighted laughter that greeted every new song, dance routine, and blackout was evidence that the "enemy" fell a willing victim.

The second part of the show struck a particularly human note that set it sharply apart from any other musical entertainment Broadway had seen. For here in words, music, dance, laughter, and sentiment Berlin re-created the rookie's life at Camp Upton. *In the Y.M.C.A.* struck a note of poignancy as a soldier sang of his haven from loneliness. There was drama too as the troops, with packs on their backs, climbed aboard ship on their way overseas.

Then Berlin himself appeared sitting in front of a pail of potatoes, and sang in his pathetic, nasal voice the rookie's complaint: *Poor Little Me, I'm A K.P.*

And, dragged out of his cot by the sharp blast of the morning bugler, he whined the lament soon echoed by every rookie in every training camp, *Oh, How I Hate To Get Up In The Morning!*

Thus a little sergeant drawing $40 a month as producer, author, actor, and composer, delivered to General Bell a check, not for $35,000, but for $80,000! And wrote two songs that swept the nation. *Oh, How I Hate To Get Up In The Morning* sold more than a million and a half copies, and *Mandy* was later incorporated in THE ZIEGFELD FOLLIES where, sung by Marilyn Miller, it created a sensation.

Out of the Army, Berlin left the publishing house of Ted Snyder in 1919 to open his own firm. From the very first, Irving Berlin, Inc. was one of the most thriving establishments in Tin Pan Alley. (It had a monopoly of the songs of Irving Berlin!)

His publishing activities did not curtail other endeavors. In the same year he embarked on an ambitious personal tour of the leading vaudeville theaters, singing his own songs at a weekly salary of $2,000.

And finally he composed the score for THE ZIEGFELD

FOLLIES of 1919 including one of his most enchanting songs, *A Pretty Girl Is Like a Melody,* and a successful carry-over from YIP, YIP, YAPHANK, the lovely *Mandy.*

Berlin was writing nation-wide hits; publishing them by the million; and singing them himself in vaudeville. No wonder he was described as the one-man trust of the song industry!

And *still* he crossed new horizons! Being a successful publisher, actor, and song composer was not enough. He became a theater owner and a producer.

Soon after returning from a Palm Beach vacation in 1920, Berlin met his old friend Sam Harris, the famous play producer. Harris reminded Berlin of something he had said casually a few years earlier: "Sam," Berlin had said, "if you ever buy another theater, call it 'The Music Box,' will you? It's such a picturesque name!"

"Do you still think 'Music Box' is a good name for a theater, Irving?" Harris asked.

"Yes, sure," Berlin said. "Why?"

"Because, Irving, you're in business. There *will* be a theater on Broadway called 'The Music Box,' and you'll be my partner."

Then Harris added: "I've just bought some property on 45th Street between Broadway and Eighth Avenue. It's an ideal spot for a show place."

Of course Berlin would join Harris in building a theater! And what a theater! A theater the like of which Broadway had never seen. A theater that would be intimate, gracious, exquisite in every detail; luxurious without being lavish; the last word in charm. His imagination fired, Berlin amplified his plans. The theater would become the home of the best musical revues theatrical genius could contrive: as intimate, as gracious, as exquisite as the theater itself. He, Irving Berlin, would write not only the words and lyrics but the entire book. The Music Box Theatre . . . The Music Box Revue . . . The idea was intoxicating. And as Berlin spoke he intoxicated Harris with his own enthusiasms.

That same fabulous attention to every detail Berlin devoted to the writing of songs, now went into his plans for the theater. Expense did not matter. Everything had to be done perfectly, regardless of cost.

Before many months passed, the wise men of Broadway—who, in the words of Oscar Wilde, knew the price of everything and the value of nothing—were making hasty computations on paper and laughing at the results. The way Irving Berlin was going, they said, the Music Box Theatre would cost a "cool million." And a "cool million" meant just this: If every seat in the theater were sold for the first five years, the owners would still have a formidable loss. This time, the wise men said, the genius who could do no wrong had slipped; and great would be his fall.

By late summer of 1921, the theater was completed, and on the evening of September 22, opened its doors to the public with the presentation of Irving Berlin's THE MUSIC BOX REVUE. Despite the high admission prices a capacity audience came to marvel at New York's most charming theater. They remained to cheer one of the brightest, most tuneful, most original musical revues they had seen. The cast included Joseph Santley and Ivy Sawyer, Sam Bernard, William Collier, Florence Moore, each a star. The musical score contained such jewels as the melodious *Say It With Music,* and the dynamic *Everybody Step.* As Arthur Hornblow wrote in his review in *Theatre Magazine,* November, 1921:

Such ravishingly beautiful tableaux, such gorgeous costumes, such a wealth of comedy and spectacular freshness, such a piling of Pelion on Ossa of everything that's decorative, dazzling, harmonious, intoxicatingly beautiful in the theatre—all that and more was handed out in a program that seemed to have no ending.

THE MUSIC BOX REVUE continued to attract capacity audiences at high box-office prices; tickets were always at a premium. And now the wise men of Broadway busily revised their estimates. By the time the show had come to the end of its magnificent run it had grossed $2,000,000. Of that sum, $400,000 was profit. Irving Berlin's "white elephant," as they had described the theater, had suddenly become fourteen-carat gold.

Four editions of THE MUSIC BOX REVUE were presented, each one among the brightest theatrical events of its year. They set a pattern of success for the Music Box Theatre. When the theater was leased to other producers, it continued as if by magic to attract one outstanding theatrical success after another, until it became known along Broadway as "the house of hits."

The MUSIC BOX Revues proved a cornucopia of wonderful Berlin melodies, a seemingly inexhaustible store: songs of magical mood, such as *Lady Of The Evening* and the enchanting *Crinoline Days;* unforgettable ballads, such as only Berlin seemed able to write, like *What'll I Do?;* novel songs like *Climbing Up The Scale;* tunes that set feet tapping and the pulse beating faster, like *Pack Up Your Sins.* No wonder they were saying there was no one in Tin Pan Alley to equal Berlin!

And Tin Pan Alley and Broadway were not alone in recognizing his powers. Even serious musicians now began paying him tribute. In 1925, the beloved Irish tenor, John McCormack, and the celebrated prima donna, Frances Alda, appeared for the first time before a radio microphone in a program of classical songs. They marked this occasion by paying homage to the great man of popular music. John McCormack sang *All Alone,* and Frances Alda sang *What'll I Do?* Berlin's songs might stem from Tin Pan Alley but they belonged to the entire world of music.

It is interesting to point out parenthetically that it was in THE MUSIC BOX REVUE that a celebrated prima donna got her start. She was a Tennessee girl who had appeared with no particular success in a few Broadway productions. Irving Berlin heard her sing and was so impressed by the quality of her voice that he engaged her for the 1924 edition of his revue. She sang *Call Of The South, Rock-a-bye Baby,* and other songs— and she "sang her way to stardom," as Alexander Woollcott noted in his newspaper column. But not even Woollcott could guess how great a star was born the night she made her debut in THE MUSIC BOX REVUE. For the young and unknown singer was destined to become one of the great opera stars of her time. She was Grace Moore.

Chapter Eleven

I'LL BE LOVING YOU, ALWAYS

ELLIN MACKAY WAS THE DAUGHTER OF wealthy Clarence H. Mackay, the head of Postal Telegraph, and belonged to the Social Register. Heiress to a fortune of $30,000,000, she had all her life known the sumptuous luxury of her Long Island estate and the association of the bluebloods of "Society."

On the other hand, Irving Berlin, son of Tin Pan

Alley and the Broadway theater, had been born to poverty in a ghetto of Czarist Russia and had lived his boyhood in the New York slums.

When Ellin Mackay and Irving Berlin were first introduced to each other in 1925, they regarded each other with the mild curiosity of two people from different worlds. They were on different social levels, with different origins and backgrounds. They were also of different religions.

They exchanged polite greetings. Ellin told Berlin how much she liked his songs.

"I've always wanted to be face to face with the man who wrote more song hits than anybody else in the world," she said softly.

"More song hits, perhaps," Berlin answered. "But, don't forget, also more failures."

He was impressed by her sensitive face and expressively animated eyes. She was so articulate, and had a ready wit. She was charming, attractive . . .

They parted company and returned to their separate worlds, perhaps never to meet again.

But Ellin was not cut to the usual pattern of the rich girl, born with a gold spoon in her mouth. Her enormous wealth brought her many things—but not the snobbery that makes it impossible to evaluate people for what they *are* rather than what they *have*. Hers was an alert intelligence, a rich culture, a natural creative gift for writing (she was later to become a successful novelist). She had interests other than clothes and jewels and luxurious living.

Irving Berlin interested her. She had known and loved his songs for many years. She considered him a genius. His ready dismissal of his accomplishments —which she recognized was not false modesty but a genuine humility—touched her. And then, the glamorous worlds of Broadway and Tin Pan Alley fascinated her, weary as she was of polite and frequently boring "Society."

She determined to know him better.

Their first casual meeting soon led to others, less casual. They began to find new depths in each other. Then, before even they realized it fully, they were in love.

Marriage was another question.

Ellin's father was proud of his social position and jealous to maintain it, and stubbornly refused to permit an alliance between his daughter and a social "inferior." He admitted Berlin's great talents and extraordinary accomplishments. But, he insisted, Berlin came from a world too far removed from his own.

Mackay told his daughter he would do everything in his power to prevent the "catastrophe" of a marriage. He engaged private detectives to follow Berlin, to know if the composer were meeting his daughter, and because he hoped to uncover information about Berlin's private life that might discredit him in Ellin's eyes. He even posted guards at his estate to prevent Berlin from gaining access to Ellin. He used every resource at his command to break up the love affair.

But Ellin was her father's daughter: she had inherited his strength of purpose and his obstinacy. She would not accept her father's superficial evaluation of human beings in terms of their social origin and background. No less resolute than her father, she would permit no one to come between herself and Berlin—not even her father. Not entreaties nor threats nor blind fury could change her mind.

At a party given at the Mackay estate in Long Island during this period, Ellin was dancing with the glamorous Prince of Wales (later the King of England who surrendered a throne for the woman he loved), at that time on a much publicized visit to this country. The Prince noted a faraway look in Ellin's eyes, and offered a penny for her thoughts. Ellin confessed that she was thinking of Irving Berlin, and poured out to her escort her tender feelings for the composer.

"This is the first time," said the Prince laughingly, "that I have had a girl dancing in my arms thinking about *another* man."

The Prince was not offended. On the contrary, he conspired with Ellin to keep her father engaged in conversation while she put through a telephone call to her lover in New York.

Realizing he was fighting a losing battle, Clarence Mackay arranged for Ellin to take a European holiday. Absence, he hoped, would bring an end to her "madness." At first Ellin refused to go. Then she consented, but only to prove to her father that separation could not change her feelings.

In Europe, Ellin pined for Berlin, thought of him continually, waited impatiently to go home. While in New York, he poured out his heart in two of the greatest ballads he ever wrote, *Remember* and *Always;* both written to Ellin, for Ellin, about Ellin.

When Ellin returned from Europe, the lovers decided that—come what may!—they would get married at once. Their plans were hatched within two hours and executed with the utmost dispatch. Secrecy had to be maintained, lest the news leak out to Ellin's father who, they knew, would stop at nothing. And the newspapers were hot on their trail!

Early on the morning of January 4, 1926, Berlin telephoned his secretary to meet him at City Hall. Ellin arrived in the first dress she could put her hands on— no wedding gown for her! Berlin came in such haste he forgot his wallet and had to borrow two dollars for the wedding license.

The ceremony took place in an atmosphere of feverish anxiety, with both bride and groom dreading discovery at any moment. Then it was over. They were man and wife, never to be put asunder.

Before the news leaked out, the Berlins went off to Atlantic City to wait the paternal blessing and forgiveness they hoped from Ellin's father. But from the great stone mansion in Long Island there came only a frigid silence. Saddened that their overtures were ignored, the Berlins set sail for a European honeymoon.

While they were gone, the newspapers had a field day with the story-book romance of a Long Island heiress and a song composer from the ghettos. A love affair that broke all social and religious barriers caught the imagination of the American public. It even inspired a song by Al Dubin and Jimmy McHugh: *When A Kid Who Came From The East Side Found A Sweet Society Rose.*

Clarence Mackay made no effort to disguise his fury. He swore he would have nothing more to do with his daughter and announced publicly that he had disinherited her. When the news reached Europe, Irving took his wife in his arms and whispered in a half-mocking tone: "My poor, disinherited darling. Now I'll have to give you a couple of millions of my own!"

For several years Clarence Mackay stubbornly refused to meet his daughter. When a girl was born to Ellin and Irving on November 26, 1926, he ignored the event completely. Two years later in September, 1928, he saw his daughter face-to-face for the first time

at the funeral of Ellin's grandmother. But he still refused to speak to her. Not even when tragedy visited
the Berlins in December, and a son died three weeks
after it was born, did he soften. In his terrible anger,
Mackay not only ignored the joy of birth but the
tragedy of death.

The economic holocaust of late 1929 swept away
most of Mackay's fortune, and finally broke his mighty
pride. For the first time he expressed the wish to see his
daughter. A reconciliation was effected at last. As he
grew intimate with Berlin, Mackay came to regard
him with genuine warmth, and not many weeks passed
after the reconciliation before he became an adoring
grandfather to the Berlin children.

As for the marriage itself, it was that Broadway
rarity, a happy consummation that, as the years
passed, only grew happier, more devoted, and more
affectionate.

For so many years Berlin had produced hit songs
and successful musical comedies (indeed, he was the
only composer who never wrote a show that failed)
that it almost seemed he could not know the meaning

of artistic frustration, or experience the bitter taste of defeat. Yet there were periods, even in a life as rich with achievement as his, when the well of inspiration suddenly ran dry. Original thoughts or pleasing melodies eluded him completely, and the old fires, that flared so hotly at the spark of a new idea, were dead. Torn with doubts about his talent, obsessed with the fear that he was through, he knew the soul-searing struggle every true artist must undergo during a period of temporary stagnation.

Such storm and stress came to Berlin one year after his marriage. In 1926, he composed three ballads that he knew were among the greatest he had ever written: *All Alone, Remember,* and *Always.* He had followed them in 1927 with three other songs, equally beautiful, and equally successful: *Blue Skies, Russian Lullaby,* and *The Song Is Ended.* Then, mysteriously —almost as if the writing of *The Song Is Ended* had been prophetic!—the vein ran out. It was as if, in writing these six gems, he had exhausted himself completely, leaving his imagination desiccated. He had not one feasible melodic idea. The more he tried to overcome his creative lethargy, the more sterile he felt;

no one had to tell him that the few songs he did write in 1928 were not only poor Berlin, but also poor Tin Pan Alley.

He was tortured by the thought that his career was now at an end. The soil that for twenty years he had planted, irrigated, and tilled so painstakingly, and that yielded such wondrous crops, was now fallow; the seeds he planted now produced only weeds.

In the past, these frustrations ended just as mysteriously as they began. When he had sadly reconciled himself to the idea that his inspiration had left him for good, a piquant melodic subject, or a neat turn of a phrase suddenly came to mind, and the old excitement of creation returned. The song assumed shape and form naturally and inevitably, and another Berlin masterpiece proved that all was well with him again.

But this time it was different.

Never before had he known such a prolonged period of artistic emptiness; never before had his struggles with himself as he tried to piece together a melody with the old Berlin magic been so harrowing. The whole year of 1929 came and went; then all of 1930; then 1931. Three terrible years of struggle!

This time he knew defeat not only within himself but outside as well. In the fall of 1929, the economic collapse laid waste to business empires and personal fortunes. It transformed Berlin from a millionaire to a pauper. He had invested his fortune in securities which, after the stock market crash, were so much waste paper.

And now that he needed his creative talent to support him, it had deserted him!

To Ellin, he said sadly: "I'm through. The song's ended for me, Ellin. What do we do now?"

"Through? Irving Berlin through?" she answered hotly. "You might just as easily say that Mt. Vesuvius is through rumbling, or the Atlantic Ocean through sending waves to the shore!"

Then she added tenderly: "You're tired, Irving. For a whole lifetime you've been writing wonderful songs, and you need a prolonged rest. You'll see, when you least expect it, the old magic will be back."

In 1932, Rudy Vallee, then at the height of his popularity as a radio "crooner," revived an old Berlin song, *Say It Isn't So,* and made it a nation-wide hit. A second old Berlin song—which the composer had neglected because he considered it inferior, but which he now issued because he had nothing else to offer—also achieved striking success: *How Deep Is The Ocean.*

With two Berlin songs in the vanguard of the hit parade, Ellin asked playfully: *"Who's* through now, Irving?"

"Ellin," Berlin answered sadly, "those songs belong to my past. I can't keep on living on the past!"

He did, however, regain enough confidence to plan with Moss Hart a new musical comedy, FACE THE MUSIC, and complete a full score. The music was by no means his best, even though the show itself was successful.

The major test, Berlin knew, was a score he was laboriously creating for Sam Harris. He could never permit himself to give Harris anything but his very best. For one thing, Harris was one of his closest friends. For another, the critics would inevitably compare the new show with the old Music Box Revues which he had produced in collaboration with Harris.

He worked alone in great secrecy; only Ellin knew how much he put into his work.

Then, for an audience of one—his wife—he played

a few of the songs he had written: *Heat Wave, Maybe I Love You Too Much, Not For All The Rice In China.*

Before Ellin could speak, Berlin said from his piano: "Here's something else I've just written for the show." And he played *Easter Parade.* . . .

Ellin did not have to say anything. She knew Berlin was himself again; and, more important still, when she embraced him and looked into his eyes, she knew that *he* knew, too.

"Maestro," she whispered, "the old magic's back!"

As THOUSANDS CHEER scored a sensational success. It had—the critics were emphatic on this point—one of Berlin's finest scores. It also had such stars as Clifton Webb, Marilyn Miller, and Ethel Waters. It rehabilitated Berlin's faith in himself completely, and provided proof to the rest of Tin Pan Alley that he was still Number One in his profession. Equally important, it rehabilitated Berlin's personal fortune. His forty per cent cut as co-producer and his royalties as composer and lyricist made him wealthy again.

Wealth and fame grew in the next few years, as Berlin went to Hollywood and wrote a succession of

ered Ethiopia and Albania, and Nazi Germany sent its armored divisions into Austria and Czechoslovakia, it became apparent that these Fascist hordes must be stopped or they would conquer and enslave the world.

The imminence of war in Europe aroused this country too. Measures were taken to make our land an "arsenal of democracy." At the same time, Americans became aware more forcefully than ever of the blessings of their own free country.

Returning from a European trip in 1938 Berlin was asked by Kate Smith, the radio songbird, for a new patriotic song to voice Americans' growing awareness of the grandeur and glory of their land. Berlin's own recent experiences in hate-torn Europe, and his delight in being back in a free America, made him eager to express his own intense love and pride in his country. He had always felt a profound debt to the country of his adoption, that never asked him where he came from, or who his ancestors were, but took him at his own worth. He wanted to repay that debt in some small measure the way he knew best, with a song.

After many painful efforts, however, he was forced to give up. He felt unequal to the occasion. He had written a lyric he thought rather good, but the proper melody would not suggest itself. Suddenly, he remembered a closing number he had written for YIP, YIP, YAPHANK in 1917, but had not used because it did not suit the occasion. He routed out the now yellow and frayed manuscript.

"I don't know if this is what you want," he told Kate Smith when he turned the song over to her. "It may not be much. But if you want it, it's yours."

When Kate had run through the score, she exclaimed: "Not *much,* Irving? Do you realize you've written the second *Star-Spangled Banner?*"

Kate Smith introduced the song over the radio, and before long, *God Bless America* became as well known to most Americans as their anthem. Through recordings the song resounded in almost every motion-picture theater. It was heard in public meeting places and sport arenas. In 1939, it was sung at the national Presidential nominating conventions of both major parties. One year later, the National Committee of Music Appreciation selected it as the best song of the year.

In England, it was given precedence over the *Star-Spangled Banner* as our national anthem because the real anthem spoke rather embarrassingly of "bombs bursting in air," in a war between America and England. In Puerto Rico, the carillon in the University Tower in Rio Piedras was wired for sound, and the song it boomed most often was a Bing Crosby recording of *God Bless America.*

Berlin allocated all the royalties—more than $100,000—to the Boy Scouts, Girl Scouts, and Campfire Girls.

From this time on, as the political tensions increased, Berlin enlisted his song-writing talent in American patriotic causes. To spur the sale of defense bonds he wrote *Any Bonds Today?* To stimulate arms production he wrote *Arms For The Love Of America.* *I Threw A Kiss In The Ocean* was inspired by Navy Relief. *The President's Birthday Ball* helped to spur the March of Dimes campaign. *Angels Of Mercy* was written to help the Red Cross. All the income from these and similar songs was donated to patriotic charities. Berlin refused to capitalize on his love for America.

Meanwhile the Nazis were on the march. Warsaw was razed. The "phony war" that followed—as the

French and German troops camped in the Maginot and Siegfried lines—erupted into a very real war. The full might of the Nazi war machine descended on helpless Belgium and France. The German air force was a black fury over England. Fortress Britain, the last stronghold of free men everywhere, absorbed every attack and stubbornly refused to yield. Seared by flame, in smoking ruins, England stood and fought with more courage than ammunition. She kept the enemy at bay. At last, after that day of infamy at Pearl Harbor, the United States gathered its prodigious strength and joined Britain. At first slowly, our defensive position was transformed into an offensive one.

Irving Berlin was too old to wear a uniform. He could, however, fight for his country in his own way. And fight he did, with complete dedication to the ideals of the struggle.

As he did in World War I, so he did in World War II. He went to Camp Upton. But this time he was no frightened and bewildered young rookie, fearing the worst, and usually encountering it. He was a man of fifty-four, world-famous, wealthy. He went voluntarily, to contribute what he could toward winning the war.

Recalling his own confusion and misery in the Army of 1918, Berlin recognized the need for entertainment of millions of young men, suddenly in uniform, far from home, and subjected for the first time to military discipline and hardship. Berlin wanted to bring into being a new YIP, YIP, YAPHANK which would, momentarily at least, provide laughter, music, and nostalgia to American soldiers everywhere.

His friends tried to dissuade him. The success of YIP, YIP, YAPHANK, they said, had been a freak; he could not expect to repeat it. Besides, they said, the army officials—up to their necks in the grim business of war—could hardly favor the expenditure of men and energy on the preparation of a show. But Berlin was stubborn.

With a portable typewriter in one hand, and a suitcase in the other, he went to live in the barracks at Camp Upton. He wanted once again to get the feel of army life, once again to meet the trials and miseries of an inductee, to come into contact with a soldier's everyday problems. A small room in the corner of the barracks, furnished with a small upright piano, became his office. After hours of aimless wandering around the camp in P-X's, service clubs, mess halls, or simply lounging with the soldiers, he worked laboriously at his script. The writing came easily. The life around him was rich with material for amusing skits, wistful or comic songs, and effective production numbers.

But if writing the show was comparatively easy, producing it was a soul-trying experience. Sifting the new Army for several hundred eligible performers was a formidable undertaking. To transfer a candidate from another service command took endless paper work, perpetual badgering of higher-ups, and considerable expenditure of time and patience. In fact, it often took so long to bring a performer from some other camp to Upton that virtually the entire show was rehearsed with understudies. It took more sweat and tears to arrange the show's tour. Service records and payrolls had to be kept moving with the men, for which a new kind of accounting machinery had to be created. Only Gargantuan effort on Berlin's part, infinite patience and tact, could overcome the problem of Army restrictions. As Berlin himself put it: "It wasn't long before I realized that I had taken on more than I could handle. But it was too late. I had the tiger by the tail and I just couldn't let go."

Eventually, perseverance won out. With the directorial assistance of Sergeant Ezra Stone, famous in civilian life for his radio characterization of Henry Aldrich, three hundred candidates were assembled from camps all over the country to form the cast, orchestra, and technical crew. Dan Healy, who had trained the dancers in YIP, YIP, YAPHANK (and who now was a night-club operator) volunteered to fill his old job. Seven others in the cast had appeared in the old show.

This was no "gold-brick" assignment: drilling and details—the bane of every soldier's existence—were not dispensed with. They supplemented arduous rehearsals which frequently continued long after other soldiers were in bed. And, regardless of how late they were up, Berlin's men were subjected to reveille, which came as relentlessly as dawn. The only additional pay a performer received—whether star or member of the chorus—was a traveling allowance of $2.30 a day, for rations on tour. The entire cast soon realized that this might be show business, but it was still the Army.

By July, 1942, Berlin's THIS IS THE ARMY was ready. The principals included Sergeant Ezra Stone, Corporal Philip Truex, Private Julie Oshins—and Mister Irving Berlin. A comprehensive coast-to-coast tour was planned, beginning with an engagement in New York City where it opened on July 4.

It was a grand show—from opening chorus to finale. As Philip Dunning, drama critic, wrote in the New York *World-Telegram,* July 5, 1942: "There will never be a service show to beat it, and it is doubtful if there will be a Broadway musical presented during the duration that will halfway approach it for sheer entertainment and wallop."

Love (*I Left My Heart At The Stage-Door Canteen*), wit (*The Army's Made A Man Out Of Me*), sentiment (*I'm Getting Tired So I Can Sleep*), broad burlesque (*Ladies Of The Chorus*), and dynamic production features (*What The Well-Dressed Man In Harlem Will Wear*) were some of the ingredients in the magic recipe.

And there was nostalgia, too. In the number preceding the finale, a melodic theme by the orchestra suddenly sent the memories of the opening-night audience plunging into the misty past. Before these memories could crystallize, the announcement came: "And now we re-create a very special scene for THIS IS THE ARMY. Let us go back twenty-five years to the Century Theatre in New York, where another soldier show, YIP, YIP, YAPHANK is playing. The curtain is going up on the second act. The scene, a barracks in Camp Upton . . ."

Irving Berlin, dressed in his Old World War I uniform, is dragged by the sergeant from his cot. Sad and a little bewildered, he sings—in that pathetic high-pitched, froggy voice of his—the old hit, *Oh, How I Hate To Get Up In The Morning*.

The song had stopped the show in 1918. And it stopped the show again in 1942.

After THIS IS THE ARMY had toured the entire country and stopped off at Hollywood to be translated to the screen, a tour of the principal cities of England, Scotland, and Ireland was planned. Berlin preceded the company in London by a few weeks, and there wrote a new song for the show, *My British*

Buddy, which struck a sentimental chord highly appreciated by the British. When the show completed its London engagement, it played in Birmingham, Liverpool, Manchester, Bristol, Bournemouth, Glasgow, Belfast—while contingents from the cast spent mornings and afternoons entertaining wounded soldiers in local hospitals. THIS IS THE ARMY left a warm glow of friendship for America wherever it played. And it realized $350,000 for British War Charities.

It was intended to disband the show after this trip. The scheduled final performance took place in London, before General Dwight D. Eisenhower. Appearing before General Eisenhower was a fitting climax: But Berlin felt no exhilaration, only sadness. There was so much good this show could yet do! Particularly for war-weary American soldiers in the fighting areas. For them THIS IS THE ARMY might be a blessed respite from dying and killing.

The performance ended, General Eisenhower warmly congratulated Berlin for his achievement. "You must be a happy man to have made such a valuable contribution to morale. If there is anything *I* can do for you, Irving, you can count on me."

"As a matter of fact," Berlin answered, "there is something *you* can do for me. You can send me and THIS IS THE ARMY to the fighting fronts."

General Eisenhower was taken aback. "There's no doubt that the show would be a wonderful tonic for the boys," he said at last. "I'll see what I can do. But remember my word is not final."

There followed for Berlin a tense period of waiting for a decision. At last, it came: an order from General George C. Marshall, the Army Chief of Staff in Washington, for a tour of all the major theaters of the war.

"You couldn't make me happier with a million bucks," Berlin exclaimed on hearing the news.

For the first time, the cast of THIS IS THE ARMY penetrated combat areas. The first stop was Italy, where American soldiers were bogged down in a relentless fight-to-the-finish with the Nazis. Enemy planes were overhead; enemy shells exploded menacingly nearby. But, in the old tradition of the theater, the show went on. Before long, the cast sang and danced and jested—oblivious of the dangers around them. A special six-hour pass was devised for the fighting G.I.'s whereby they could leave their foxholes by truck, see the show, and then return to their fighting. There was no doubt that this brief respite from war brought these tired soldiers renewed courage and hope.

The show traveled north from Naples, appearing in Rome five days after the city was liberated. In Rome —at a civilian performance at the Royal Opera House, for the benefit of Italian war orphans—Berlin introduced another new song, *There Are No Wings In A Foxhole.* This scored such a success that, in response to the ovations, Berlin sang several of his old-time favorites. And he concluded with a popular Italian song, *Oh, Marie,* which he had learned as a boy on the streets of New York's East Side and which, tactfully, he sang for his audience in Italian.

From Italy, the cast traveled on to Cairo, then to the devastating heat of Persia. By now it had encircled half the globe and there loomed before them the Pacific area—a long and laborious trip to Australia, and from there to New Guinea, the Admiralty Islands, the Philippines, the Netherland East Indies, the Marianas, the Caroline Islands, Saipan, Okinawa. . . . Evenings were given up to performances. Mornings and afternoons were spent in hospitals. Berlin himself was no less active than the youngest member of his troupe. At hospitals, he frequently officiated as master-of-ceremonies, principal comedian, and singer of ballads —all three rolled into one. He gave of himself, his energies, his talents unsparingly.

On the evening of October 22, 1945—in Honolulu —THIS IS THE ARMY gave its last performance. It had traveled around the world over a period of three years and three months. It had entertained two-and-a-half million G.I.'s. It had brought in more than $10,000,000 for the Army Relief Fund.

For his unstinting and tireless contribution to the war effort, Berlin was decorated by General Marshall with the Medal of Merit.

Berlin not only wrote the war's best show in THIS IS THE ARMY, and the war's best patriotic song in *God Bless America,* he also created the war's most poignant sentimental song.

In 1942, he had sold to Metro-Goldwyn-Mayer a story originally intended for a lavish Broadway musical and which he now adapted as a screen vehicle for

Bing Crosby and Fred Astaire. Called HOLIDAY INN, its ingenious plot revolved around a vacation resort; the story called for a song about every major American holiday. For the Christmas season, Berlin wrote a ballad, *White Christmas,* which not only became the most successful number of the entire score, but one of the most successful Berlin songs in many years. In the first four months it sold a million copies of sheet music (it had been quite a number of years since a popular song could sell a million copies!) and close to two million phonograph records. By the end of the first year, these figures were trebled. Since then, *White Christmas* has become as much a classic in American popular song literature as *Easter Parade.* It now seems unthinkable to celebrate the season of holly and mistletoe without listening to this tender melody.

A success of such proportions, while certainly welcome, was nothing new to Berlin. *White Christmas* would have been for him just another resounding hit in a life studded with resounding hits—but for one vital difference. The turmoil of the times in which it appeared gave it a significance quite apart from its popular appeal.

To the Pacific, where, inch by inch, American soldiers were fighting their way through savage jungles infested with insects, filth, malaria, and the enemy, *White Christmas* came as a blessed reminder of happier days in happier places. Attacked more violently by their homesickness than by their fear of either disease or the Japanese, these boys found in this ballad sweet memories of home. Singing it made life in the heat and the swamps just a bit more endurable. Through all the battlefields of the Pacific, the men sang *White Christmas* as they sang no other song, because in singing it they felt themselves, momentarily, brought a little nearer home.

Chapter Thirteen

A MAN WHO WROTE SONGS

BERLIN IS A VERY LITTLE MAN. SHORT, spare, slight of build, he gives a first impression of insignificance. Nor is he an impressive conversationalist. He speaks in clipped phrases, generously spiced with slang. He is not particularly good company. Quiet, introspective, often self-conscious, he prefers to hide behind a shell of reticence. When he talks he comes right to the point, usually without subterfuge or even tact. Then he suddenly lapses into silence. You get the uncomfortable feeling that you have been obliterated.

His face almost always wears an expression of worry. As he looks at you (sometimes out of tortoise-shelled glasses), his soft, brown eyes are touched with sadness. You also notice soon enough that he is all nerves. He seems to be continually driven by forces he is incapable of stemming. His movements are abrupt and brisk, whether he is talking, gesturing, or pacing the room. Even when he is deep in conversation his hands move nervously all the time: play with a cigarette; stroke his naturally curly hair; remove and replace his glasses; punctuate his remarks with a swift movement of wrists. When he works he smokes one cigarette after another, chewing gum as he smokes; at frequent intervals he jumps up from his desk or piano to pace the room. He seems incapable of relaxation, does not know the meaning of repose. You feel, as you watch him, that he generates as much energy as a dynamo.

So much for the impression Irving Berlin makes on a stranger. How do his friends see him?

They see him, of course, as a genius, and are in awe of the almost casual way he keeps on producing little masterpieces and million-dollar successes. But they also see him as a magnificent businessman who knows how to exploit his genius. They know he can drive as hard a bargain as anyone; and they respect him for it.

Most people who know him only casually complain of his icy reserve, and of his complete self-absorption. But his close friends know he is warm and affectionate —with a generous, sentimental streak a mile wide. They know his heart and his pocket are wide open to those in need; he is one of Broadway's easiest "touches." It is not generally known (except to those intimate with him) that he has forgotten none of his old associates from the Bowery of long ago. For one of them he opened a charge account in the neighborhood grocery store; for another, he defrayed hospital expenses; for a third, he provided money for a small business; for a fourth, he assumed funeral costs. Most often these gifts (and they are numerous) are made without the recipients knowing who their benefactor is.

Hobbies play no important part in his life. The man

doesn't seem to know the meaning of play. He used to indulge in an infrequent game of poker, but since he did not find much fun in gambling, he dropped it. Sometimes he plays a round of golf, but with no particular enthusiasm. Occasionally he cooks a meal for his family or friends and experiments with unusual recipes. During the Italian tour of THIS IS THE ARMY he cooked all the meals for those quartered with him. But he cooks rarely. Recently he has turned to painting, but his participation in this pastime is thus far spasmodic.

The truth is, that outside his own family, his interest is all centered in his work. With a relentless drive that gives him no rest, he is often involved in several projects at once. And when he is not working, he is bored.

And yet it cannot be said that he *likes* working. It would seem that, having composed a thousand songs, some among the most beautiful in American literature; having written the scores for twenty Broadway shows, all successful; and having achieved an eminence in his field no one can hope to challenge, he should have supreme confidence in himself. But every time he undertakes a major work he is assailed by tormenting doubt and uncertainty. He feels he'll never have another good idea for a song. He begins to suffer stomachaches and headaches. The lines on his face grow deeper. The sadness of his eyes becomes more poignant. His friends watch his agony and say: "Irving is giving birth to another million-dollar hit."

But though it costs him unspeakable anguish, his work absorbs all his interest. All his waking moments, ideas for new lyrics, new melodies, a new piece of show business are spinning wildly in his head, and like the colors of a kaleidoscope, trying to arrange themselves in a workable pattern. (Perhaps this accounts for his reticence in company.) And though physically he may be at the Colony in New York (his favorite restaurant) enjoying its exquisite dishes with the zest of a gourmet, or attending a swank party as an honored guest, or playing the gracious host in the living room of his fashionable home in New York, or resting at his fifty-two-acre farm near Livingston Manor in the Catskill Mountains, he is actually working—all the time.

His method of working is as extraordinary as the results it achieves.

It is well known that America's foremost song composer does not know how to read or write music. He cannot even play the piano properly: he knows only one key, F-sharp major, and has a special lever under the keyboard of his piano with which he can transpose music into any desired key. With instinct as his only guide, he works out a melody, every bar costing him sweat and tears. He walks nervously up and down his room developing an idea, rushes to the piano to try out a phrase, then resumes his pacing, as the idea grows, expands, develops. When, finally, a song is clearly crystallized in his mind, he plays it for his musical secretary, who puts it down on paper. The secretary plays the song ten times, twenty times, sometimes even fifty times, as Berlin makes revisions.

He always writes the words to his own songs: his melodic genius sometimes obscures the fact that he is also one of the most original and graceful lyric writers in the song industry. He has often said that lyrics are more difficult for him than melody. A random idea, a catch phrase, a happy slogan, a neatly turned idiom, a fleet rhyme is the germ to infect him. In a fever of creation he slaves to develop the idea into a complete

143

lyric, and to reduce it to such simple words and such economical phrasing that it acquires a charming air of spontaneity through its very simplicity.

Generally speaking, he writes the words first, and allows the lyric to dictate the appropriate melody. He types the lyric with one finger, then holds the copy in his hand, reading and rereading it aloud until "the first thing I know I begin to get a sort of rhythm, then a tune. I don't say all my songs are written that way, for sometimes I hear a tune first, and then start fitting words to it. In either case, whichever part comes first, serves as a mold into which the other must be poured." He is by no means satisfied with his way of writing songs. Painfully conscious of the fact that he is musically illiterate, he has an exaggerated respect, even awe, for musicians who can sit down and write a complicated orchestration as easily as they write letters. He is always amazed to hear these same learned musicians speak of him with veneration and even, on occasion, use the terrifying word "genius." He winces. In his heart of hearts he cannot quite escape feeling that it was luck, and only luck, that produced his thousand songs, and that he himself actually had very little to do with it.

This modesty is no pose. He is incapable of putting on airs, or adopting false attitudes. Yet—make no mistake about it!—he is as proud of his triumphs as he is of his family; and he is as much in love with his best songs as he is with his wife and daughters.

On occasion he allows himself the indulgence of retrospection. In reviewing his career, he singles out six major events that were milestones:

1915—the performance of WATCH YOUR STEP, the first time a complete musical score of his was heard on Broadway . . .

1918—YIP, YIP, YAPHANK . . .

1919—his first complete score for THE ZIEGFELD FOLLIES . . .

1921—the first MUSIC BOX REVUE . . .

1933—As THOUSANDS CHEER, a show that lifted him permanently out of his prolonged doldrums . . .

1943—THIS IS THE ARMY . . .

And as memory allows the parade of his thousand songs to file past, he singles out from this parade eight that he considers the greatest he has written:

Alexander's Ragtime Band . . . *I Love A Piano* . . . *Always* . . . *Say It With Music* . . . *A Pretty Girl Is Like A Melody* . . . *Easter Parade* . . . *God Bless America* . . . and *White Christmas.*

Chapter Fourteen

I'M ALL ALONE

BERLIN'S EARNING POWER HAS ALWAYS
been prodigious. In 1947 for instance his Broadway
show, ANNIE GET YOUR GUN, was the outstanding
theatrical attraction of the year, from which he drew a
weekly income of about $2,500 in royalties. In addition,
Metro-Goldwyn-Mayer had bought the show for
$650,000, one-third of which was his. His latest
motion picture, EASTER PARADE, for which Metro had

paid him close to $600,000, was packing first-run motion-picture theaters. At the same time, second-run theaters were playing BLUE SKIES, released in 1946, bringing him 12½ per cent of the gross.

His publishing house with exclusive rights to all his songs earned more than a million dollars during this year. Berlin was also drawing royalties from the sale of phonograph recordings of his songs, possibly another $250,000; an annual income from his membership in ASCAP of $20,000; and from his part-ownership of the Music Box Theatre in New York.

No wonder the wits of Broadway say: "Who says the world's gold is buried at Fort Knox? It's in Irving Berlin's vault."

Certainly no one ever received such fabulous financial returns from writing music. And, one suspects, if there should arise anybody in the future to equal or surpass Irving Berlin, that man's name will be—Irving Berlin. For in Hollywood, on Broadway, in Tin Pan Alley—wherever songs are made, sung, and sold—Irving Berlin has set the pace so far ahead of all his competitors, that he now walks from one major triumph to the next, unrivaled—alone, all alone. . . .

As he contemplates the extent of his success, unique in American music, Irving Berlin must often permit himself the luxury of reminiscence. At such moments, he must bring back to mind times when he was less fortunate. The terrifying day when, hiding under a blanket in the fields, he saw smoke and flames envelop his town of Temun. . . . The exhilarating moment when he joined his brothers in the queue to his mother's apron to deposit there the first few pennies he had earned, selling papers. . . . The frightening hours when, after having run away from home, he experienced cold, hunger, and uncertainty. . . . The thrill of holding in his hand a copy of his first published song, *Marie from Sunny Italy*. . . .

And in reflecting on these, and other similar, episodes of the distant past, more than once must Berlin have spoken three words of which he was the author: *"God Bless America!"*

Not merely enormous sums of money, but many honors and tributes have come to Irving Berlin.

In 1943, the National Association for American Composers and Conductors (an organization that concerns itself only with serious music, incidentally) acknowledged Berlin's unique place in American music when it presented him with a citation as this country's "outstanding composer of popular music."

Richard Rodgers—the composer of OKLAHOMA, SOUTH PACIFIC, and other celebrated musical-comedy scores—and his collaborator, Oscar Hammerstein 2d, honored Berlin on his sixtieth birthday by establishing the Irving Berlin Scholarship at the Juilliard School of Music for talented young musicians.

John Alden Carpenter, the American composer of serious music, wrote: "I am strongly inclined to believe that the musical historian of the year 2000 will find the birthday of American music and that of Irving Berlin to have been the same."

Many things have been said and written about Berlin in an attempt to give the measure of his stature. Jerome Kern, another of America's great composers of popular songs, said: "Irving Berlin has no place in American music. He *is* American music." Alexander Woollcott, the celebrated writer, raconteur, and critic, wrote: "He is—really there is no other word which accounts for him—a genius."

And yet—what well may be the most fitting verbal garland to place on his shoulder is an epigram invented not for him, but for another genius of song, Franz Schubert. This tribute came from the lips of Schubert's beloved friend, Holzapfel. And as we try to find the encomium which will best pay honor to Irving Berlin, we might aptly echo these tender words of Holzapfel about Schubert:

"He was a very little man. But he was a giant."

APPENDIXES

1
THE MOST FAMOUS SONGS OF IRVING BERLIN

2
BROADWAY PRODUCTIONS
FOR WHICH BERLIN WROTE THE SCORE

3
MOTION PICTURES
FOR WHICH BERLIN WROTE THE SCORE

4
SELECTED RECORDINGS OF BERLIN'S
MOST FAMOUS SONGS

THE MOST FAMOUS SONGS
OF IRVING BERLIN

1909: *That Mesmerizing Mendelssohn Tune; My Wife's Gone to the Country* (with Whiting and Snyder)

1910: *Alexander and His Clarinet; That Beautiful Rag* (with Ted Snyder)

1911-1912: *Alexander's Ragtime Band; Everybody's Doin' It; That Mysterious Rag; That Ragtime Violin. You've Built a Fire Down in My Heart* (from JARDIN DE PARIS)

1913-1914: *When I Lost You; When The Midnight Choo-Choo Leaves for Alabam'*

1915-1916: *I Want to Go Back to Michigan; That International Rag. Simple Melody, What Is Love,* and *When I Discovered You* (from WATCH YOUR STEP). *I Love a Piano* (from STOP, LOOK AND LISTEN)

1917-1918: *This Is the Life; When I Leave the World Behind. Oh How I Hate to Get Up in the Morning,* and *Mandy* (from YIP, YIP, YAPHANK)

1919: *You'd Be Surprised. A Pretty Girl Is Like a Melody* (from THE ZIEGFELD FOLLIES of 1919)

1920: *Girl of My Dreams,* and *The Syncopated Vamp* (from THE ZIEGFELD FOLLIES of 1920)

1921: *All By Myself. Say It With Music,* and *Everybody Step* (from MUSIC BOX REVUE, first edition)

1922: *Some Sunny Day. Crinoline Days, Pack Up Your Sins, Dance Your Troubles Away,* and *Lady of the Evening* (from MUSIC BOX REVUE, second edition)

1923: *The Waltz of Long, Long Ago,* and *What'll I Do?* (from MUSIC BOX REVUE, third edition)

1924: *Lazy; All Alone*

1925: *Always; Remember*

1927: *Blue Skies; Russian Lullaby; The Song Is Ended*

1929: *Puttin' on the Ritz* (from PUTTIN' ON THE RITZ)

1930: *Reaching for the Moon* (from REACHING FOR THE MOON)

1932: *Say It Isn't So; How Deep Is the Ocean. Let's Have Another Cup of Coffee,* and *Soft Lights and Sweet Music* (from FACE THE MUSIC)

1933: *Easter Parade,* and *Heat Wave* (from As Thousands Cheer)

1935: *Cheek to Cheek,* and *Isn't This a Lovely Day* (from Top Hat)

1936: *I'm Putting All My Eggs in One Basket,* and *Let's Face the Music and Dance* (from Follow The Fleet)

1937: *I've Got My Love to Keep Me Warm*

1938: *God Bless America. Now It Can Be Told* (from Alexander's Ragtime Band)

1939: *It's a Lovely Day Tomorrow,* and *You're Lonely and I'm Lonely* (from Louisiana Purchase)

1942: *White Christmas* (from Holiday Inn). *I Lost My Heart at the Stage-Door Canteen* (from This Is The Army)

1946: *You Keep Coming Back Like a Song* (from Blue Skies). *They Say It's Wonderful, Doin' What Comes Natur'lly, Show Business,* and *The Girl That I Marry* (from Annie Get Your Gun)

1947: *It Only Happens When I Dance With You,* and *Fella With an Umbrella* (from Easter Parade)

1949: *Paris Wakes Up and Smiles, Homework, Little Fish in a Big Pond,* and *Let's Take an Old-Fashioned Walk* (from Miss Liberty)

BROADWAY PRODUCTIONS
FOR WHICH BERLIN WROTE THE SCORE

1911: JARDIN DE PARIS

1914: WATCH YOUR STEP

1915: STOP, LOOK AND LISTEN

1918: YIP, YIP, YAPHANK

1919: THE ZIEGFELD FOLLIES of 1919

1920: THE ZIEGFELD FOLLIES of 1920

1921: MUSIC BOX REVUE (first edition)

1922: MUSIC BOX REVUE (second edition)

1923: MUSIC BOX REVUE (third edition)

1925: MUSIC BOX REVUE (fourth edition); THE COCOANUTS

1927: THE ZIEGFELD FOLLIES of 1927

1931: FACE THE MUSIC

APPENDIXES

1933: As Thousands Cheer

1939: Louisiana Purchase

1942: This Is The Army

1946: Annie Get Your Gun

1949: Miss Liberty

MOTION PICTURES
FOR WHICH BERLIN WROTE THE SCORE

1929: THE COCOANUTS; PUTTIN' ON THE RITZ

1935: TOP HAT

1936: FOLLOW THE FLEET

1937: ON THE AVENUE

1938: CAREFREE; ALEXANDER'S RAGTIME BAND

1939: SECOND FIDDLE

1942: HOLIDAY INN

1943: THIS IS THE ARMY

1946: BLUE SKIES

1947: EASTER PARADE

1950: ANNIE GET YOUR GUN

SELECTED RECORDINGS OF
BERLIN'S MOST FAMOUS SONGS

NOTE—*The letters introducing order numbers denote Victor (V),*
Columbia (C), and Decca (D).

SINGLE DISCS	Record No.
Alexander's Ragtime Band	
—Bing Crosby and Al Jolson	D-40038
—Benny Goodman and Orchestra	V-25445
(See also albums: VP-159; CC-78; DA-656)	
All Alone—Joan Edwards, Paul Whiteman and Orchestra	D-2691
(See also albums: CC-78; DA-70; DA-654)	
All By Myself (See album: DA-481)	
Always	
—Grace Moore, RCA Victor Orchestra	V10-1171
—Eileen Farrell and Orchestra	D-23366
—Dinah Shore and Orchestra	V45-0010
—Guy Lombardo and the Royal Canadians	D-23817
(See also albums: VP-159; CC-78; CM-784)	
Anything You Can Do—Bing Crosby, Dick Haymes, and Andrew Sisters	D-40039
(See also albums: VC-38; DA-468)	
Blue Skies	
—Frank Sinatra, Tommy Dorsey and Orchestra	V-27556

Blue Skies (continued) — Record No.

—Bing Crosby, Chorus and Orchestra — D-23646

—Dinah Shore and Orchestra — V-450007

—Perry Como, The Satisfiers, Russ Case and
  Orchestra — V-201917

(See also albums: VP-159; CC-78; DA-481)

Cheek To Cheek—Nat Brandwynne and Orchestra — D-24075

(See also album: DA-654)

Crinoline Days—Paul Whiteman Woodwinds — D-2694

(See also album: DA-70)

Doin' What Comes Natur'lly

—Jimmy Dorsey and Orchestra — D-18872

—Glenn Hughes, Freddy Martin and Orchestra — V-20-1878

(See also albums: VC-38; DA-468)

Easter Parade

—Bing Crosby and Orchestra — D-23819

—Eddy Duchin — C-35705

—Perry Como and Orchestra — V-202142

—Guy Lombardo and Royal Canadians — D-23817

(See also album: CM-784)

Everybody Step (See album: DA-481)

Fella With An Umbrella—Bing Crosby and
  Orchestra — D-24433

The Girl That I Marry—Dick Haymes and Orchestra — D-23780

(See also albums: DA-468; VC-38)

	Record No.
God Bless America	
—Bing Crosby and Orchestra	D-23479
—All American Orchestra, Stokowski	C-17204D
—Deanna Durbin and Quartet	D-18675
—Horace Heidt and His Musical Knights	C-35637
Heat Wave—Charles Baum Orchestra	D-24066
(See also album: DA-656)	
How Deep Is The Ocean	
—Carmen Cavallero	D-24060
—Dinah Shore and Orchestra	V-45007
(See also albums: DA-70; CM-784)	
I've Got The Sun In The Mornin' (See albums: DA-468; VC-38)	
I Left My Heart At The Stage-Door Canteen (See album: DA-340)	
It Only Happens When I Dance With You— Guy Lombardo and Royal Canadians	D-24434
I Want To Go Back To Michigan (See album: DA-656)	
Lady Of The Evening—Paul Whiteman and Orchestra	D-2690
(See also albums: CC-78; DA-70; DA-654)	
Let's Take An Old-Fashioned Walk (See albums: CM-860; CML-4220)	
Little Fish In A Big Pond (See albums: CM-860; CML-4220)	
Mandy—Ted Streeter and Orchestra	D-24010
Oh, How I Hate To Get Up In The Morning (See album: DA-340)	

Record No.

Paris Wakes Up And Smiles (See albums:
  CM-860; CML-4220)

A Pretty Girl Is Like A Melody
  —Andre Kostelanetz and Orchestra   C-4267-M
  —Alec Templeton   C-36164
  —Bob Grant and Orchestra   D-24020
  —Kenny Baker and Orchestra   V-26664
  (See also album: VP-159)

Puttin' On The Ritz—Harry Richman and Orchestra   D-24391
  (See also album: DA-481)

Remember
  —Dinah Shore and Orchestra   V-450009
  —Kenny Baker and Orchestra   V-26664
  —Asa Harris, Erskine Hawkins and Orches-
  tra   V-201639
  (See also albums: VP-159; CC-78; CM-784;
  DA-70)

Russian Lullaby—Guy Lombardo and Royal
  Canadians   D-23762
  (See also album: DA-70)

Say It Isn't So (See album: DA-654)

Say It With Music
  —Paul Whiteman and Orchestra   D-2690
  —Carmen Cavallero   D-24016
  (See also albums: VP-159; DA-70; DA-654;
  CC-78; CM-784)

APPENDIXES

165

Record No.

You Keep Coming Back Like A Song—Dennis
    Day, Russ Case and Orchestra   V-201947
    (See also album: DA-481)

You'd Be Surprised—Eddie Cantor and Orches-
    tra   D-23987

You're Lonely And I'm Lonely—Mary Martin
    and Orchestra   D-23151

ALBUMS   Record No.

ANNIE GET YOUR GUN
    —Audrey Marsh, Maxine Carroll, Jimmy
    Carroll, Earl Oxford, The Mullen Sisters,
    with Al Goodman and Orchestra   VC-38

Contents

*They Say It's Wonderful; I Got Lost In His
Arms; You Can't Get A Man With A Gun;
Doin' What Comes Natur'lly; The Girl That
I Marry; Who Do You Love, I Hope; Moon-
shine Lullaby; I've Got The Sun In The
Mornin'.*

    —Ethel Merman, Ray Middleton, Original
    Cast, Chorus, Orchestra   D-468

Contents

*Doin' What Comes Natur'lly; Moonshine
Lullaby; You Can't Get A Man With A Gun;*

*I'm An Indian, Too; Anything You Can Do;
They Say It's Wonderful; I Got Lost In His
Arms; I've Got The Sun In The Mornin';
The Girl That I Marry; My Defenses Are
Down; Show Business; Who Do You Love,
I Hope.*

BLUE SKIES
—Bing Crosby, Fred Astaire, Orchestra and
Chorus   DA-481

Contents

*Blue Skies; I'll See You In C-U-B-A; You
Keep Coming Back Like A Song; Getting
Nowhere; A Serenade To An Old-Fashioned
Girl; Everybody Step; All By Myself; I've
Got My Captain Working For Me Now;
A Couple Of Song And Dance Men; Puttin'
On The Ritz.*

IRVING BERLIN MELODIES
—Nancy Evans, Earl Randall, Wayne King
and Orchestra   VP-159

Contents

*Always; Blue Skies; All Alone; Say It With
Music; Remember; A Pretty Girl Is Like A
Melody; What'll I Do?; Alexander's Ragtime
Band.*

Record No.

IRVING BERLIN SONGS
—Joan Edwards, Clarke Dennis, Paul
Whiteman and Orchestra   DA-70

Contents

*Say It With Music; Lady Of The Evening;
All Alone; Remember; How Deep Is The
Ocean; Russian Lullaby; Crinoline Days;
Tell Me, Little Gypsy.*

—Risë Stevens and Orchestra   CM-784

Contents

*Say It With Music; How Deep Is The Ocean;
Always; Easter Parade; They Say It's Wonderful; Remember.*

—Dick Haymes, Carmen Cavallero   DA-654

Contents

*Say It With Music; The Song Is Ended;
Cheek To Cheek; Say It Isn't So; Soft Lights
And Sweet Music; The Girl On The Magazine Cover; All Alone; Lady Of The Evening.*

—Andrew Sisters, Vic Schoen and Orchestra   DA-656

APPENDIXES

Contents

Alexander's Ragtime Band; I Want To Go Back To Michigan; Heat Wave; When The Midnight Choo-Choo Leaves For Alabam'; Some Sunny Day; How Many Times.

MISS LIBERTY

   —Eddie Albert, Allyn McLerie, Mary Mc-Carty and Original Cast, Chorus and Orchestra

CM-860
CML-4220

Contents

Overture; I'd Like My Picture Took; The Most Expensive Statue In The World; Little Fish In A Big Pond; Let's Take An Old-Fashioned Walk; Homework; Paris Wakes Up And Smiles; Only For Americans; Just One Way To Say I Love You; You Can Have Him; The Policeman's Ball; Falling Out Of Love Can Be Fun; Give Me Your Tired, Your Poor.

MUSIC OF IRVING BERLIN

   —Al Goodman and Orchestra

CC-78

Contents

Lady Of The Evening; Say It With Music; Blue Skies; Remember; Say It Isn't So; All Alone; Always.

Record No.

THIS IS THE ARMY
  —Original All-Soldier Cast, Chorus and
  Orchestra   DA-340

Contents

*Overture; This Is The Army; I Left My Heart
At The Stage-Door Canteen; Oh, How I Hate
To Get Up In The Morning; How About A
Cheer For The Navy; American Eagle; With
My Head In The Clouds; What The Well-
Dressed Man In Harlem Will Wear; The
Army's Made A Man Out Of Me; I'm Get-
ting Tired So I Can Sleep.*

INDEX

INDEX

INDEX

INDEX